"Several things endeared me to *Unburdened* [...] use of contemporary versions of Scripture, a [...] drawn from real lives lived in community. A[...] the reader to ponder thoughtfully and practic[...]ally the exercises suggested by the author. This is a book worth buying for personal use and to give away. I highly recommend it."

LUCI SHAW, poet and author of *The Generosity* and *Eye of the Beholder*

"Jesus calls to himself those who are weary and burdened, promising to give them rest, saying that his yoke is easy and his burden light. This beautifully honest book about the promise and demands of forgiveness is a Lenten companion to those words, conveying Christ's rest for our many burdens."

JONATHAN TRAN, associate dean for faculty in the Honors College and associate professor of theology at Baylor University and the author of *Asian Americans and the Spirit of Racial Capitalism*

"Jesus offers us life, abundant life, which is a lifelong journey of unburdening. That's the Lenten experience made available to us in these pages. Carol Penner guides us down the path of repentance and forgiveness as we confront the powers of sin in us and around us, all as part of our lifelong pilgrimage into the wonders of grace, of grace upon grace—the endless grace of God's life with us."

ISAAC S. VILLEGAS, ordained minister and contributing editor for the *Christian Century*

"The forty-day spiritual trek we call Lent is too often a solitary journey inward in self-exploration. This book offers a journey back to failures, outward to co-travelers, and forward in a search for forgiving, reconciling, and reconstruction of relationships. I suspect that the teacher Jesus would like this book even more than I do since it fulfills his vision of what real spirituality is truly about. Carol Penner is a trustworthy guide for this walk of renewal through reunion with others."

DAVID AUGSBURGER, professor emeritus of pastoral care and counseling at Fuller Seminary School of Theology and author of *The Freedom of Forgiveness* and *Caring Enough to Confront*

UNBURDENED

A
DAILY
DEVOTIONAL

CAROL PENNER

UNBURDENED

A LENTEN JOURNEY TOWARD FORGIVENESS

HERALD
PRESS

Harrisonburg, Virginia

Herald Press
PO Box 866, Harrisonburg, Virginia 22803
www.HeraldPress.com

Library of Congress Cataloging-in-Publication Data
Names: Penner, Carol, 1960- author.
Title: Unburdened : a Lenten journey toward forgiveness (a daily
   devotional) / Carol Penner.
Description: Harrisonburg, Virginia : Herald Press, [2024] | Includes
   bibliographical references.
Identifiers: LCCN 2023039497 (print) | LCCN 2023039498 (ebook) | ISBN
   9781513813585 (paperback) | ISBN 9781513813592 (ebook)
Subjects: LCSH: Lent--Prayers and devotions. | Devotional calendars. |
   Forgiveness--Religious aspects--Christianity. | BISAC: RELIGION /
   Christian Living / Devotional | RELIGION / Christian Living / Spiritual
   Growth
Classification: LCC BV85 .P38 2024 (print) | LCC BV85 (ebook) | DDC
   242/.34--dc23/eng/20231016
LC record available at https://lccn.loc.gov/2023039497
LC ebook record available at https://lccn.loc.gov/2023039498

Study guides are available for many Herald Press titles at www.HeraldPress.com.

UNBURDENED
© 2024 by Herald Press, Harrisonburg, Virginia 22803. 800-245-7894. All rights reserved.
Library of Congress Control Number: 2023039497
International Standard Book Number: 978-1-5138-1358-5 (paperback); 978-1-5138-1359-2 (ebook)
Printed in United States of America

28 27 26 25 24   10 9 8 7 6 5 4 3 2 1

For Louisa

Contents

Shrove Tuesday

Bear fruits worthy of repentance. —Luke 3:8

READ: Luke 3:7–14

Sin is a burden. For some it's hefty, and we feel it sitting on our chest from the moment we wake up. For others, it's merely a pesky weight that we carry on our back, and we may hardly notice that it drags us down.

Our smaller sins catch up to us. Tiny straws added one by one can form a backbreaking load. I criticize a family member instead of offering a kind word. I turn away from the person who is homeless, and then don't give money to the homeless shelter, like I intended. I leave the church meeting in a huff because people didn't like my idea. Things we did or didn't do pile up, sins of commission or omission. At times memories of these sins can descend upon us with a vague uneasiness; are we actually being the person we want to be?

The effects of our bigger sins can be harder to avoid. I betrayed a friend. I hit someone. I stole something valuable from someone. Through my negligence, someone was harmed. Or we are part of bigger systems of sin. I consider my lifestyle and see my huge carbon footprint. My white ancestors settled North America, and I have benefitted from the continuing racism against Indigenous peoples.

We might feel remorse or grief, or perhaps we just feel like we are in limbo because we don't know how to address the damage done. We seek forgiveness from God, but we still live with these broken relationships.

We are also burdened by harm done to us; sometimes this burden is something we shoulder our whole lives. Maybe you were abused by a family member. Maybe your best friend was killed by a drunk driver. Maybe your spouse broke their marriage vows to you or a business partner cheated you financially. Because of the color of your skin, maybe you experienced the thousand cuts of racist remarks. Perhaps you witnessed the atrocities of rampaging soldiers and fled your country. Or maybe the parent who was supposed to love and nurture you was cruel and manipulative.

When we are hurt, we may experience emotions like rage and resentment toward the person or system that harmed us. While our suffering varies in degree and duration, every human being lugs around pain; we have to figure out what to do with it. People may encourage us to forgive, but doing so can seem beyond us. Are we stuck carrying hatred and anger forever?

Lent is the period of forty days before Easter when we think about letting go of the burden of sin. Lent is a time to orient ourselves toward Easter and the possibility of new life in Jesus Christ. It's a time to journey toward giving and receiving forgiveness.

We follow Jesus on this path toward forgiveness. God's forgiving love came in the form of a baby, incarnated for us. Jesus asked God to forgive those who harmed him. His resurrection is a testament of the power of that love, because God can rescue us even from death.

This book is not titled *Forty Easy Steps to Achieve Forgiveness.* Forgiveness is wild and elusive, and it can take our whole lives to forgive those who harmed us. Sometimes we may never manage it. And when we have caused harm, we may deeply and earnestly desire forgiveness from others, but we may not receive it. We cannot control whether people forgive us.

Forgiveness is both a gift from God and it's the hardest work we have to do. In these pages, we will be encouraged to take small steps toward freedom, toward forgiveness.

Today is Shrove Tuesday, the day before Lent. The verb *shrove* is rarely used anymore. It's a religious word—to be shriven means to confess your sins and be forgiven. *Shrove* is both active and passive; there are things we need to do and things we need to receive to be shriven.

In denominations where priests receive a person's confession, being shriven is straightforward. You confess to the priest and are assigned something to do to show your penitence. The priest, in their sacramental role, assures you that your sins are forgiven. It's more vague in Protestant denominations. Some churches have prayers of confession in each worship service, but many do not. Confessing and receiving forgiveness is often considered to be entirely private, an exchange between you and God. Yet as we will consider in the coming forty days, there is work to be done to make our repentance visible.

We learn about the first step toward forgiveness from John the Baptist. People flocked to see him to hear his call to "a baptism of repentance for the forgiveness of sins" (Luke 3:3). He also instructed, "Bear fruits worthy of repentance" (v. 8). John expected visible signs of repentance in the life of a repentant person. He gave specific instructions to the tax collectors, the soldiers, and the crowd.

When I was a teenager considering the decision to be baptized, I reflected on the call to repentance. I couldn't really think of too many bad things I had done. Little things here and there, certainly, but *repentance* seemed like too big of a word for that. I remember praying, "God, help me see where I need to repent."

Well, God is faithful, and that may be the most answered prayer I've ever prayed! The older I've grown, the more clearly I see where I've gone wrong. It's humbling to hear how my own angry words and thoughtless actions have harmed others. It's been even more challenging to understand how I'm part of larger systems and structures that are doing harm.

I teach at a university now where I am surrounded by young people. For many years I was a pastor working in a congregation where many people were older than me. In both of these communities, I heard stories of repentance, and saw the fruit it could bear.

What does the fruit of repentance look like in my own life? That's something I'm working on steadily both individually and with my church community. I will share some of these stories in the weeks ahead. Thank you for joining me on this journey! On this day, and every day through Lent, we will pray together, asking for God's help.

> **PRAY:** *God of hope, where can we find you?*
> *We wander in wildernesses,*
>   *only faintly hearing a voice calling us to freedom.*
> *You know the details of the burdens on our backs.*
> *You know the harm we've done,*
>   *the haunted histories we've inherited,*
>   *and the wounds we carry.*
> *They are a dead weight, and a weary load.*
> *We are so accustomed to bearing it,*
>   *we can't even imagine life without this strain.*
> *In this season of Lent, walk with us.*
> *Guide our steps to the places you know,*
>   *to rivers in the wilderness,*
>   *and refreshment in unexpected places.*
> *We long to taste the freedom you offer*
>   *through Jesus Christ our Lord. Amen.*

FOR REFLECTION

Consider where you are right now when it comes to forgiveness. Is there a burden you are carrying? Do you have people you want to forgive, or are you seeking forgiveness from someone that is a long time coming? Perhaps you know people who are on journeys like these. In these stories, does God seem close or far away?

Notes on the Road Ahead

As you journey with this book, here are some things to consider:

Scripture texts: I've chosen some familiar biblical stories about forgiveness, as well as some passages that are not typically associated with forgiving. I encourage you to read the scripture text in full because it can speak to us in surprising ways.

My context: I share a variety of stories from my own life and an eclectic mix of stories that people have shared with me along the way. To protect identities, some details have been changed in the stories; when only a first name is used, it is a pseudonym. The notes section at the end of the book includes published sources where you can read more about particular stories. I am writing as a person in the Mennonite tradition. Mennonites and other Anabaptists place a strong emphasis on community and listening for God's voice in the gathered group of believers. You can expect to read not only stories of individuals navigating sin and forgiveness, but of communities as well.

A note about content: To talk about forgiveness, we need to talk about sin, and some of the stories I share here cover sensitive topics, including child abuse, domestic abuse, sexual assault, racial violence, and murder. Painful experiences have many different facets. Some of the stories may resonate with you, and some may not, because your context and life experiences are different. I don't intend for the stories I share to be prescriptive; forgiveness takes many forms within the church.

Prayer and reflection: Each daily reflection concludes with a prayer, which I hope will be useful as you turn to God with your own words. You will also find questions for reflection. These prompts are meant to help you reflect on your own life, whether by writing in a journal or musing with your own thoughts. My hope is that these devotions are a launching place, not an ending place. It's my prayer that this book will draw us all closer to one another and to God.

Small group study: If you are reading this book with someone else, there is a guide for small groups at the back with helpful questions and additional prayers. These questions often parallel the ones in the daily reflections, and you may find it fruitful to share your answers with companions on the road.

WEEK 1

SEEKING
REPENTANCE

Searching for Forgiveness

So I say to you, Ask, and it will be given to you; search, and you will find; knock, and the door will be opened for you. —Luke 11:9

READ: Luke 11:1–13

This passage in Luke begins with the disciples asking Jesus to teach them to pray. He gives them a short prayer, which we call the Lord's Prayer. It includes the line "Forgive us our sins, for we ourselves forgive everyone indebted to us." I learned this prayer as a child because my father said it with my siblings and me every night before we went to bed. In our version we said, "Forgive us our trespasses, as we forgive those who trespass against us."

Where in the life of Jesus does this prayer come? A few chapters before, in Luke 9, Jesus tells the disciples that he is going to suffer, be rejected, and killed. Then he says, "Let these words sink into your ears: The Son of Man is going to be betrayed into human hands" (Luke 9:44).

Jesus has seen crucifixions before. He can imagine his future suffering perfectly. Jesus is living with this harsh reality that awaits him—it has sunk into him. It is in this context that he teaches the disciples about prayer, and forgiveness is top of mind.

I am a Mennonite, which means I belong to a Christian denomination that is part of the Anabaptist tradition. Anabaptism originated in the 1500s in Europe. This reform movement encouraged people to follow Jesus and to make an informed choice to be baptized. Congregations are at the center of community life, the place where we read Scripture together and discern God's voice.

Anabaptists are a part of the peace church tradition, which believes Christians should not respond violently to violence. Anabaptists also emphasize forgiveness. In congregational and family life, conflict is a constant. As a young person growing up in the church, I don't remember any discussion of justice, but I do remember people talking about letting things go and forgiving people even if they had not apologized. I heard stories of persecution of early Anabaptists who were killed in terrible ways but forgave their persecutors. We were encouraged to forgive like the martyrs did. These stories sank into me in a deep way.

A contemporary story of forgiveness I've heard in church numerous times happened in the Amish community of West Nickel Mines, Pennsylvania. In 2006, a man with a gun entered an Amish school, took hostages, and then shot numerous schoolgirls, killing five. Representatives from the Amish church immediately and publicly forgave the perpetrator (who died by suicide after the shootings), and they reached out to his family with compassion. This remarkable, forgiving response of a community to a horrific crime became news around the world. I've heard this story recounted from the pulpit with awe as an example of how we should respond to violence.

Stories that are less famous, but also important, also need to be told. Torah Bontrager grew up in an Amish community where she experienced terrible physical and sexual abuse. She talks about young women forced to publicly ask their abusers for forgiveness because the church believed that the women had tempted the men to sin. Both the survivor of abuse and the person who raped her were punished with excommunication for six weeks, after which no one was allowed to talk about what had happened. Bontrager was tempted to kill herself because she felt so trapped. Instead she escaped her community and now has written about her horrible experiences.[1]

These are two stories about forgiveness from the same Anabaptist tradition. One story is held up as a model for us to follow, but the other is barely heard. Churches of all denominations have miraculous forgiveness stories, and they have also used the call to forgiveness to silence hurting people, keeping them in vulnerable positions where they could be hurt again.

These are extreme stories on the forgiveness spectrum. Many of our own stories fall somewhere in between. We don't have to look far to find examples of where we need forgiveness. As I think about my own extended family, I can immediately think of half a dozen grudges and hard feelings that have festered and grown for years. Maybe your own family story is similar. We long for resolution.

Many years ago, our seven-year-old daughter was playing in my husband's office while we were working outside. We were surprised when two fire trucks and an ambulance came rolling up with sirens and lights. We explained there was no emergency. My daughter insisted she had not called 911. That night she went to bed early because she said she had a stomachache.

I went and talked to her, and in the dark she confessed that she had called 911 and had hung up immediately. "I didn't know they would come if I didn't talk to them," she said. She made a mistake, but by covering it up she felt a secret was weighing her down. Her confession and my assurances helped her find peace. Many of us long fervently for that kind of peace to the larger problems that we face.

We have a promise from Jesus in Luke 11:9 that if we ask questions about forgiveness, we will be given some answers. If we search diligently, God will show us the way. We are one knock away from God's presence. Let's venture onward together with forgiveness on our minds.

PRAY: *Jesus, we've learned about forgiveness in word and deed,*
    and it's not always been good news.
When we've been badly hurt,
    our pain was sometimes discounted:
    churches expected us to forgive
    at the expense of our own safety.
When we've hurt others, chasms opened so deep and wide
    that forgiveness can seem unattainable and unrealistic.
Can you offer us life in this desert?
Can you offer freedom in places where we feel desperate?
You lived without hatred and taught us new ways.
Today, we ask for help as we seek forgiveness in our lives.
We are diligently searching for it.
We pray for open doors
    and the courage to walk through them. Amen.

FOR REFLECTION

When you think about forgiveness in today's world, what stories come to mind? Are these examples of people extending forgiveness or withholding it? Which stories are you more likely to hear in church?

THURSDAY

Embracing Belovedness

So she named the LORD who spoke to her, "You are El-roi," for she said, "Have I really seen God and remained alive after seeing him?" —Genesis 16:13

READ: Genesis 16:1–16

Hagar was an enslaved person, the lowest of the low on the power ladder in her society. We don't know anything about her history other than that she was Egyptian. Why was she in Canaan with Abram and Sarai and so far from home? Was she captured in a raid or sold to repay a debt? We do know she was displaced and alone, far from the family and people who could have protected her.

Hagar was forced to work for Sarai. She had no say when Sarai told her to go and have sex with Abram. She could not consent; she was enslaved.

At a certain point, Hagar decides she can't take it anymore. She runs away with her son in tow even though she is putting both of their lives in danger. There in the wilderness, Hagar meets an angel who tells her that God has plans for her and her child, promising they will prosper. Hagar responds by naming God El-roi, "the God who sees me." She is the first person in Scripture to give God a name.

Many people are bothered by the fact that the angel tells Hagar to go and submit to Sarai. Why does the "escape plan" that the angel offers require returning to her abusers? Why couldn't God have led Hagar to a promised land of her own?

I wonder what Sarai's reaction was to this runaway. Stories of slavery I know from other contexts suggest that Hagar would not have been greeted with welcoming arms upon her return. Did the abuse stop or intensify? We aren't told how that part of the story unfolds. What we do know is that the Hagar who went into the wilderness is not the same Hagar who comes back. Now she knows that God is watching her and has promised great things to her and her son. Sarai is no longer the most powerful force in Hagar's life.

This isn't a Bible story that people normally use to explain forgiveness, because forgiveness isn't an explicit part of the story. The angel doesn't say to Hagar, "Forgive Sarai." But there is a great truth in this story that affects our ability to forgive. God sees our pain, especially the pain of the neglected, the downtrodden, the powerless, and the overlooked. God sees the lonely tears and hears the anguished cries, the moans into pillows. God has hopeful plans even for enslaved Hagar.

When people hurt others, they often objectify them and treat them as less than human. That is the very basis of enslavement or abuse. It is very common for hurt people to absorb that objectification and to think badly of themselves, sometimes believing that they deserve the abuse.

I wonder if that was Hagar's reality. I can imagine Sarai screaming at her, "You worthless slave!" Imagine hearing that not once, but for years on end from everyone around you. Hagar realizes in the wilderness that she is worthy of God's notice. She is no longer defined by the people who abuse her.

Perhaps the most important step toward forgiving those who harm us is this kind of reorientation to take away the power from them. Instead of being an object, we are now the beloved. When we know that belovedness in our soul, perhaps only then can forgiveness begin to dawn on the horizon.

I think of a friend whom I will call Therese. From the time she was a child, Therese's mother physically and emotionally abused her. I imagine little Therese cowering in her room, with nowhere to turn, and with no one to help her. She had years of suffering ahead, and she could not imagine a life without her mother hurting her.

How do people in such dire situations receive a message from God? What saved my friend Therese? When she went to church as a young adult, the community welcomed her and embraced her. They taught her that she was a beloved child of God. When Therese felt safe enough to tell her story to members of the church, they said, "We hear your pain. This was wrong, this should not have happened. We will help you get through this." The community was an angel of God for her.

The people in the church who heard her story were sensitive enough to not say, "Therese, you should forgive your mother." Instead, they sat patiently with Therese in her pain and sorrow. It took years for the stories of abuse to trickle out. They cherished her. She felt loved.

Did the church members hope that Therese would reach a place of forgiveness for her mother? I am sure that in their minds it was a hope. But they knew that talking about forgiveness too soon would lay a heavy burden on Therese when she was already carrying so much. She might have felt judged and inadequate; she might have felt that she didn't belong in church because she wasn't ready to forgive.

I wonder how my own church can be a place of healing for those who have been badly hurt. Are we willing to sit with people in their grief and love them? There are no detours around this part of the forgiveness journey.

PRAY: *Jesus, you reached out to so many who were ignored.*
You saw the disabled person who could not get into the pool,
the man with leprosy cast out of society,

the woman caught in adultery, about to be stoned.
You knew the Scriptures, and heard the story of Hagar,
*   alone, friendless, and enslaved.*
You embrace us when we are distraught and dismissed
*   and have nowhere else to turn.*
We don't want to be people who see a hurting person
*   and walk by on the other side.*
We are sure to find you when we pause to accompany
*   those whom you put in our way. Amen.*

FOR REFLECTION

Have you experienced someone putting you down or criticizing you continually? If the criticism happened for an extended period, how did that affect your self-identity? Did faith in God help you along the way?

FRIDAY

Turning Around

Then the son said to him, "Father, I have sinned against heaven and before you; I am no longer worthy to be called your son." —Luke 15:21

READ: Luke 15:11–32

When we think of Bible passages that deal with forgiveness, this parable of the father and the prodigal son may immediately spring to mind. I've heard so many sermons on it, and the emphasis is mostly on the father's forgiving actions, his open arms, and loving attitude. Yet in the gospel of Luke, this parable is linked with the parables of the lost sheep and the lost coin, stories that are about repentance. Jesus refers to "joy in heaven over one sinner who repents" (Luke 15:7). The prodigal son has not only seen but felt the error of his ways in his empty belly. His lifestyle has left him impoverished, and in the environment of the pigsty he has found time to think about the meaning of his actions.

The son isn't coming home saying, "I have nowhere to go, and I'm poor, will you take me in?" He does not announce, "I've run out of money." That would be a simple, limited appeal to his father's pity. Instead, the son has realized the error of his ways. Having disrespected his father by asking for an early inheritance, and after using the money to exploit prostitutes, he says, "I have sinned against heaven and before you." The son returns home repentant. The father may have embraced the son even without repentance; it's hard to say. However, Jesus tells the story in the context of teaching about repentance.

The Greek word translated as "repentance" in this story, *metanoia*, means a fundamental change in thinking that leads to changed behavior. Repentance is not just sharing an idea about change, but a change in actions. Repentance is always about more than our words.

Repentance was central to Jesus' teaching. Shortly after his baptism and the forty days in the wilderness, Jesus begins to preach, "Repent, for the kingdom of heaven has come near" (Matthew 4:17). He did not mean that people should only think in their heads, "I've done something wrong." Jesus implored people to change the way they behaved.

When we get caught doing something wrong, there can be many emotions. We can feel bad for lots of reasons. I may feel bad because I was caught, or I may wish I hadn't made that mistake, because now I'm facing the consequences. I may feel bad because I am in trouble. Repentance is something different; it requires something deeper and it takes more time.

I once hurt a friend by saying something very critical about her behind her back. The remark made its way back to my friend, and she confronted me. I felt bad immediately, because it cast me in a bad light that I would talk about someone that way. Initially, I was most worried about my own damaged reputation. True repentance about what I said came more slowly. When I saw the pain my words had caused, I started to empathize with my friend. Over time, acknowledging the pain I caused helped me reflect on my own character and why I had acted that way. Repentance turned me around. I had apologized for what I did almost immediately after my friend called me out, but repentance happened as I gained empathy and became more careful about the words I said going forward.

Repentance that only uses words is shallow. Take, for example, repentance from the great sin of racism. A white person like me can say, "I'm sorry I was racist," but my actions will show whether I truly have repented and changed. For those of us who benefit from whiteness, repenting of racism means that we need to listen carefully to Black people and other people of color when they explain their experiences of racism. It means not only stopping our own prejudiced acts and remarks but also becoming more aware of our privilege. It can mean using our power to advocate for the oppressed when we see racism at work. Repentance is not a one-time event, but an ongoing change in direction, with the opportunity for continual course corrections. We live in a context where racism is commonplace, and the road to unpack that legacy in my own heart and actions is long and hard.

The Truth and Reconciliation Commission of Canada, or TRC, was a public forum from 2008 to 2015 where Indigenous peoples could name the harm done to them for all to hear. I participated in some of these meetings. We were on holy and painful ground as we listened to the devastating stories of children who were abducted from their parents and forced into residential schools where they were abused in many ways. These boarding schools were funded by the Canadian government, and many were administered by churches. Listening to the stories was the first step toward accountability.

I have never been part of a gathering where there were so many tears. People just cried and cried. One ritual that surrounded this storytelling session was that at the end of each session, the wet tissues were collected and then ritually burned in a ceremonial fire, with the smoke offered to the Creator. Tears were sacred in this space.

Many recommendations came out of the TRC; unfortunately, Canada has been slow to follow them. Our repentance has not really borne much fruit yet. But some recommendations are being implemented, like changing the curriculum in public schools to include teaching about residential schools. This way the next generation will learn about the harm done, and it's a way of holding Canada accountable. We show we are repentant when we take responsibility for the harm we caused.

PRAY: *Holy Spirit, you great whirlwind,*
   blow into our lives and turn us around.
For those of us who have experienced racism,
   thank you for your presence here with us.
You hear every remark and see every put-down;
   you grieve the burden of systemic discrimination we carry.
For those of us who are shielded by whiteness as privilege,
   show us our destructive ways,
   and open our eyes to the pain we cause.
Help us listen, help us learn, help us turn.
You are the way—teach us to follow you. Amen.

FOR REFLECTION

Consider a time when you realized you did something wrong. What emotions did you experience, and how long did they last? Can you think of an example of a group or an organization realizing it did something wrong? How did it respond? What happens when no one takes responsibility for harm?

SATURDAY

Taking Responsibility

The man said, "The woman whom you gave to be with me, she gave me fruit from the tree, and I ate." —Genesis 3:12

READ: Genesis 3:1–13

God calls in the garden, "Where are you?" Adam and Eve are hiding silently among the trees because they did precisely what God asked them not to do. The story invites us to imagine their panic—they don't want to have to explain what they've done.

Who wants to admit they made a mistake? Certainly not Adam. He blames Eve for his actions, "She is the one who caused this problem." Adam doesn't want to take responsibility. Perhaps Eve doesn't want to either.

Some time ago, I backed my car into a tree as I was leaving a church that I was visiting. My car jerked to sudden stop with a loud smash, and shocked, I jumped out to survey the scene. At the edge of the parking lot there was a row of trees in a line. One tree was two feet in front of all the others—the one with my bumper wrapped around it. When I told the story to my family, I drew their attention to the stupidity of the person who planted those trees. I avoided taking responsibility for the collision. I had been careless; it was my responsibility to watch where I was driving, and I failed. I didn't want to carry the weight of what I'd done.

Around the time I hit that tree, a man in my church (whom I will call Evan) sexually abused a young person in the neighborhood.

Evan was actually caught doing this crime. When confronted about the obvious abuse, he blamed the child.

Many people in our church were very angry because Evan was not taking responsibility for his actions. I, too, was angry with him. I spoke with a counselor who specialized in working with people who sexually abuse children. The counselor explained that no one wants to admit to abusing a child. There is such a stigma attached to this crime that people who commit the crime will seek someone or something else to blame. Most people who abuse children have a story in their mind explaining why it's not their fault, or why the transgression is supposedly okay. It often takes months if not years of counseling for the perpetrator to unpack that story and tell the truth, laying the blame where it belongs.

Our church faced a crisis when Evan was arrested and released on bail pending a trial. Would we allow him to come to church? Some said that he could attend only if he admitted what he did was wrong. Basically, they wanted him to stay away and be alone until he figured out how to be repentant. Others thought that we should walk alongside Evan and offer the help he needed to pick up the heavy burden of the harm he caused.

And then I hit the tree. I saw that even though our mistakes were on very different scales, neither I nor Evan wanted to take responsibility. We each came up with a story to show how the wrong we committed wasn't our fault.

The stories we tell when we do bad things can be quite far-fetched. I know of several church leaders who sexually abused people in their care. Each one had a story to justify the abuse. "I'm in love with my congregant." "My job is so hard, and I deserve this." "Lots of leaders do things like this; we can't be perfect."

Leaders who violate boundaries sometimes tell stories that involve God. "God says this is OK." "God wants us to do this."

"Most people are not supposed to do this, but it's OK for us, because God has revealed a new ethic that only I understand." They misuse the power given to them as a spiritual leader to mislead a vulnerable victim.

I knew an elderly person in my church who was robbed by her grandson. She was in the hospital and had given her debit card to him to pay some bills. When she got out of the hospital, she found that a substantial amount of money was gone from her account. What story did the grandson tell himself when he stole the money? "Grandma would probably give me this money if I asked her." "Grandma is going to leave me some money in her will, so I'm not stealing it; I'm just taking what's mine." But his actions caused material harm to his grandmother, who now had to borrow money to pay her next month's rent.

We choose to hurt people, and Adam-like, we resist and shift responsibility. We leave destruction in our wake.

Denial is a burden in itself. We may feel free initially because we aren't shouldering the responsibility for what we've done. But lying to ourselves is a weight that should never be underestimated. I remember sitting with someone who, after long years of denial, suddenly felt the weight of the harm she had caused. It was crushing, and even more crushing because of the time spent evading the truth. She wept as if the weight of the world was upon her.

But as in the story with Adam and Eve, God is looking for us. We can think we are hidden, but God knows what we've done and wants us to repent. Clarity is God's Spirit working with us, showing us the invisible chains we've forged that are weighing us down. Every lie forms a link in the chain, every evasion of responsibility is a weight that pulls us down. God can help with the unburdening, but we first have to admit we've done wrong. Taking responsibility: this is our Lenten journey.

PRAY: *God, you know the hoops we jump through,*
the elaborate stories we tell,
the three-ring circus we conjure.
We jump up and down, pointing to everyone else,
but you know the truth.
We can't hide from you.
Thank you for helping us when we hide from ourselves.
Call us to account for the way we've used our power
to hurt others and benefit ourselves.
Give us ears to hear your call in the garden. Amen.

FOR REFLECTION

Can you think of a time when you made excuses for something you did or failed to do? What story did you tell yourself and others who were affected by the situation? Did you eventually take responsibility for your actions? If not, are you ready to take responsibility today? How do you see God working?

SUNDAY

Practicing Penitence

Now on the twenty-fourth day of this month the Israelites were assembled with fasting and in sackcloth and with earth on their heads. —Nehemiah 9:1

READ: Nehemiah 9:1–17

In the Hebrew Bible (what Christians call the Old Testament), repentance is a common theme. However, it's usually not individuals who are being called to repentance, but the whole people of Israel as a group.

In the scripture passage today, the people have come to an understanding of their sins. They have a rush of understanding and then a grief that cannot be contained. It flows out of them with their loud cries; they can't pretend it's just life as usual. The tide of repentance floods into their life, and everyone will see this sea change. They put on sackcloth.

In the ancient Near East, it was common to let your grief show. This might be counterintuitive for those today who place a high value on keeping up appearances. Maybe you can think of a time when you felt really upset about something, but you put on a brave face and went about your day, hoping that people wouldn't notice what was going on inside your head.

Wearing sackcloth was the exact opposite of keeping up appearances; it was the equivalent of waving a flag of grief for everyone to see. Sackcloth was a simple rough cloth made of goat hair, as recognizable as it was uncomfortable. When someone was wearing sackcloth, they were in a crisis. It was a sign of penitence.

Penitence is another word that we do not hear very often today. It carries layered meanings, such as being repentant and wanting to show you are sorry by your actions. A prison is sometimes called a penitentiary. At least theoretically, convicted criminals are put in prison to repent of their crimes.

What does penitence look like? In England in the year 1200, King Henry II made a terrible mistake. He felt bothered by the archbishop of Canterbury, Thomas Becket, who wasn't doing what the king wanted. King Henry II commented to his knights about how much this archbishop was bothering him. The knights took the king's words seriously and they rode to Canterbury. They found the priest in the cathedral and they killed him right in front of the altar.

The whole of England was scandalized by the king's actions. Would the people even follow a king who would dare to kill an archbishop? In response, the king repented of his actions. To show that he was repentant, King Henry II walked barefoot to the cathedral and, kneeling at the door, asked the monks, some of whom had witnessed the murder, to beat him.

Was Henry II sincere in his repentance, or was this showmanship to get the people of England on his side? Only God knows. But the king certainly knew that to convince people of his repentance, he would need to do more than say a private prayer and believe he was forgiven. He needed to show his sincere repentance to the people around him. This is called penitence.

In 2006, I was in Ukraine for the dedication of a monument to the thirty thousand Mennonites who disappeared after they were arrested by Josef Stalin's government in the 1930s. This is just a small fraction of the enormous number of people killed by Stalin. The stone monument shows silhouettes of a man, a woman, and two children. Matthew 5:4 is written on the base of the monument in Ukrainian, Russian, German, and English: "Blessed are those who mourn." Mennonites funded this statue with full cooperation from the Ukrainian government. The Ukrainian government, in addition to participating in the dedication, also opened up archives to allow researchers to look for information. Families could finally find an answer about when and where their loved ones died.

The memorial that we dedicated that day did not erase the pain of those disappearances, but it is an example of penitence, a public form of repentance. It was a way of saying, "This should not have happened, and we don't want it to happen again."

I contrast this act of penitence with the biblical story of the pharaoh of Egypt in Exodus. He abused the people of Israel by enslaving them, and he initially ignored the call of God to let them go. He eventually says the right words and seems to repent: "This time I have sinned; the LORD is in the right, and I and my people are in the wrong" (Exodus 9:27). But a few verses later he again refuses to let the people leave. His repentance didn't get any deeper than his lips. It certainly did not reach his heart.

I was raised in a Protestant tradition where the idea of penitence was not emphasized. I was taught that if I sinned, I should close my eyes and pray silently to God about it, and I would be forgiven. I never heard a lesson about confessing sins out loud to someone else. Sackcloth has fallen out of fashion even in church.

I wonder whether we can personally carve out a place for penitence in Lent. Is there something you've done that is weighing on your conscience? Maybe you have talked to God about it. But have you ever told another human being about what you've done and what you plan to do differently? Confession to another person is a penitential act. Who might you share with and what might you do to show you're repentant?

PRAY: *Jesus, are you listening?*
In my still, small voice I can find the courage
  to admit to you the wrong I've done.
But when I think of anyone else finding out about it,
I quake inside. It would mean the image
  I've carefully constructed for those around me
  would crack and crumble.
But that's how your light gets in.
Give me courage to tell one person,
  someone who will not excuse what I've done
  but will hold me accountable,
  so it doesn't happen again. Amen.

FOR REFLECTION

Think about a time when you felt filled with grief and repentant about something you did. Considering the discussion and examples given above, would you say you were truly *penitent* as well? If you were raised in the Christian church, what were you taught about the process of forgiveness? Was receiving forgiveness mostly about you and God, or was there an outward element?

MONDAY

Focusing on Fasting

While they were worshiping the Lord and fasting, the Holy Spirit said, "Set apart for me Barnabas and Saul for the work to which I have called them." —Acts 13:2

READ: Acts 13:1–5

In the Hebrew Bible and the New Testament, we see people fasting as they listened for God. They gave up certain types of food or certain meals, or they removed themselves to lonely places. Fasting is a form of self-discipline. Every time you crave the thing you miss, it calls you to prayer. The important thing is not what you are giving up, but rather the orientation toward God.

Fasting has long been associated with Lent, when we reflect on Jesus' passion as well as our sins. Perhaps you know someone who has given up something for Lent. I know people who have given up chocolate, or coffee, or something technological like social media for a period of forty days. If trusting in God is a place you are trying to reach, fasting is a vehicle to help take you there.

Irena Sendler was a young Polish woman who worked in the Resistance to the Nazis in World War II. She was a devout Christian, and she believed that she was called to help those in trouble. She always carried with her a small card that said, "Jesus, I trust in you."

At the risk of her life, her network smuggled twenty-five hundred Jewish children out of the Warsaw Ghetto before they could be deported to death camps. Sendler kept careful records of the names of the children and their parents and the homes where they were hidden.

Sendler was eventually caught and imprisoned. In her cell, she had no Bible but only the small card saying "Jesus, I trust in you." As she experienced interrogation and torture, she never revealed the location of the archive of the children's parents or the identities of other Resistance members.

I think of Sendler in the prison cell, where so much had been taken from her—her liberty, her friends, her possessions, her autonomy over her body. She had only that small scrap of paper. And in that place of extreme deprivation, God met her. On the day Sendler was to be shot, God miraculously provided an escape, although she would carry the scars of her imprisonment for the rest of her life. In prison, Sendler wasn't fasting voluntarily; although deprivation was forced upon her, her trust in God solidified.

In my early adulthood, I learned about a sad story from my own family. My paternal grandparents were new immigrants to Canada, and they clung to their own cultural group, maintaining their language and traditions in this new environment. All my father's family married people from this particular cultural group, but my father fell in love with someone from a different group. He knew his parents wouldn't approve, so he eloped with the woman he loved. He came home and told his parents he was married.

They would not forgive him. They were so furious with him that they said they would not meet his new wife. They refused to meet my mother for years until my oldest sister was born, at which time our family was reluctantly let back into the fold.

I wonder what that forced exclusion was like for my mother, shunned from joining a family because she had a different cultural heritage. The distrust and abandonment undoubtedly added to marital tensions, and when I was two years old, my parents split up.

My family did not talk about this messy story. I didn't hear about it for years, because when I was four years old, my mother died, and the grandmother who had excluded her welcomed my sisters and me into her home for four years until my father remarried. I had warm feelings toward this grandmother, who died when I was twelve. When I first heard this painful story as an adult, I was filled with anger and bewilderment toward my grandmother. How could she have acted so horribly? How could someone who was so generous to me be so ungenerous to my mother?

As I reflect on my family history, with these deep valleys of unresolved hurt, I am struck by how deeply my family needed the practice of fasting and giving something up. Not the practice of giving up food, but of giving up grudges. Giving up anger. Giving up prejudice. Turning to God and remembering that we are all God's beloved children.

I wonder whether my grandmother ever regretted her actions toward my mother. I never heard that she gave anyone an apology. But perhaps in her decision to care for me and my sisters, she worked out her regret through positive actions. I know she had a deep Christian faith, and I remember seeing her reading her Bible every day. I am inspired by Sendler's story and her little card. Jesus, I trust in you. God is working in ways we cannot always fathom.

Churches in North America are dividing over so many different issues. Money, LGBTQ+ inclusion, women in ministry, and politics. People on both sides of an issue condemn the other side. The fruit of this judgment is not love, joy, and peace but loss, violence, and fractures in the church. What if instead of arguing over this or that interpretation of the Bible, we decided to participate in a communal fast from hatred of each other? Could "Jesus, I trust in you" be our motto?

Perhaps you have given up something for Lent already or have been thinking about doing so. When we fast, the longing for that thing will remind us to pray, or will free up time for us to do so. In our longing for God, we are sure to meet the one we are seeking.

> **PRAY**: *God, we show our devotion in different outward ways;*
>   *you see our hearts, and our sincere longing for you.*
> *When we have unresolved hurts,*
>   *you are with us as we tell the stories of our lives.*
> *We trust that you will, in your good time,*
>   *deliver forgiveness into our lives,*
>   *a gift that sets us free.*
> *We pray all this in the name of Jesus,*
>   *who is truly trustworthy. Amen.*

FOR REFLECTION

Think of a time when your life was pared down to more simple circumstances, whether voluntarily or involuntarily. How was this an opportunity to meet God? If fasting is something you have done before, what was that experience like? If you have never fasted, is there anything that intrigues you or concerns you about trying it?

TUESDAY

Dying to Self

Work on your own salvation with fear and trembling, for it is God who is at work in you, enabling you both to will and to work for his good pleasure. —Philippians 2:12–13

READ: Philippians 2:2–13

In our scripture today we glimpse the road that Jesus was asked to walk, a road of obedience. He wasn't being called to be obedient to the authorities around him who had lots of rules: "Don't heal on the Sabbath; don't associate with tax collectors and sinners." Jesus was obedient only to God.

Another way of describing obedience is "dying to the self," giving up one's own way, and letting God take control of the direction of one's life. Augustine of Hippo was a church leader and theologian in Northern Africa. In the year 400 CE, he wrote an autobiography of his early life called *Confessions*. He describes in personal detail the process of giving up control to God. He did not want to give up his life of sinful pleasures, so his prayer in those early years was, "Give me chastity . . . only not yet."[2]

Augustine observes how reluctant we humans are to be obedient to God. He tells the story of his friend Alypius, who wanted to be faithful but was continually drawn to the Colosseum to watch the blood sports, where prisoners were forced to fight to the death. It was an addictive pastime that Alypius struggled mightily to give up. But being obedient to Jesus meant leaving that all behind.

As Christians, we are called to give up our grudges and carefully kept scores. We can become obsessed with getting even, as if it were a blood sport. Too often we think, "Make me pure, but not yet." We want to put someone in their place, or to get revenge in some way, and *then* we'll follow Jesus. But obedience to Jesus means following now, not in some future time. It means trying to replace vengeance with compassion.

Being yielded to God does not mean being a doormat for others. Sometimes obedience to God means challenging those in power and calling them to account. Martin Luther, the great Protestant Reformer, critiqued the Catholic Church instead of remaining obedient to it. He believed that God was calling him to a new reading of Scripture and to new practices in the church. Luther nailed his critique to the door of the church in Wittenberg in 1517. For the next three years his superiors pressured him to recant. He wrote, "My conscience is captive to the Word of God. . . . God help me. Amen."[3]

Rosa Parks was not obedient to the racist laws in Montgomery, Alabama, when the bus driver told her she was sitting in a seat reserved for white people. She refused to move and was arrested. In solidarity with her, thousands joined a bus boycott to protest discrimination. Obedience to God can mean believing in your right to exist with equal rights to other human beings. It can mean disobedience to those who exploit you. Yieldedness to God can set us on a collision course with authorities in this world.

As I am writing this, smog from forest fires in Canada has blanketed the eastern part of North America. Climate change, with its high temperatures, drought-like conditions, and intense electrical storms, has led to one of the worst fire seasons in recorded history.[4] Many today are questioning the unbridled use of fossil fuels. It's just one aspect of our sinful treatment of the natural world. We continue to contaminate the land, the air, and the water.

What does obedience to God look like in the face of environmental sin? For me, it means being more careful about reducing, reusing, and recycling. I think carefully about whether I need to fly somewhere. I've recently rediscovered a cookbook I received in the 1980s as a wedding present, the *More-with-Less Cookbook*. The author, Doris Janzen Longacre, thinks carefully about the theological value of simplicity and how it is worked out through our dietary choices. She suggests that our everyday small purchases of food affect not only our own bodies, but the world around us. I appreciate the challenge to act locally and think globally.

For too long, churches ignored efforts to conserve natural species and spaces, thinking that environmental care was a secular pursuit. Now, when the world faces an unignorable crisis made by human hands, churches must start to think differently. Repentant words are shallow unless they are accompanied by actions.

The college where I work, Conrad Grebel University College, motivated by its Christian values, has established an environmental committee that is determined to reduce our carbon footprint. Our first steps were simple: Can we recycle more garbage and turn off more lights? The next steps cost more money: Can we replace these leaky windows? Can we install a more energy-efficient heating and cooling system? Now more ambitious projects are being explored, including the installation of solar panels and the capture of heat from a six-foot sewage tunnel that runs through our property. Pursuing an environmentally responsible life is not easy. Too often our prayer is, "God, make us environmentally careful, but not yet."

In my experience, one of the hardest places to be obedient to God, and to die to the self, is in congregational life. We each want our own way, whether that is deciding which minister we hire, how we spend the church budget, or selecting the color of the new carpet in the sanctuary. Sometimes we wish that people we find difficult would just leave the church. It can be hard to embrace the diversity of the body of Christ. Because the Holy Spirit is working within us for God's pleasure, we can be confident that change is possible. We can work to build up the body of Christ rather than just pursuing our own way.

PRAY: *God, we repent of how we have overconsumed*
and overproduced,
overusing the world's resources again and again.
We have been overconfident in the inexhaustibility of nature.
We confess that the wealthy (many of us),
are overrepresented in overconsumption.
We have overreached and overstepped,
and the consequences are overwhelming.
God, undergird us as we remember who you created us to be.
Jesus, we understand your call to humility and obedience.
Holy Spirit, as we undertake new directions
with our families, our churches, and communities,
we know that you will be with us
no matter what we undergo. Thank you.

FOR REFLECTION

What is your relationship to the word *obedience*? Have you ever felt God calling you to do something you really didn't want to do? If you listened to that call and responded with obedience, why did you do so?

WEEK 2

ADDRESSING SIN

Lamenting Harm

But Tamar put ashes on her head and tore the long robe that she was wearing; she put her hand on her head and went away, crying aloud as she went. —2 Samuel 13:19

READ: 2 Samuel 13:1–21

The story of Tamar is a story of sexual assault, heartbreak, and shattered dreams. This text from 2 Samuel is referred to as a "text of terror" by biblical scholar Phyllis Trible.[5] After she was raped by her brother, Tamar might have gone away quietly to hide and suffer in silence. Many people who experience sexual assault don't tell anyone.

Tamar chooses to go public with her grief instead. She puts ashes on her head, she tears her long robe, she puts her hand on her head and wails. She has the power to tell her story. Like many survivors in the #MeToo movement today, she will expose the bad that was done to her. She doesn't fade away quietly.

I am struck by the way that power permeates this story. The men wield power in destructive ways. Amnon and Jonadab plot and entrap. Amnon rapes. The male servant throws Tamar out and bolts the door. All the men use their power to do harm.

King David, the person with the most power in this story, hears what happened and does nothing. He does not appear to have one shred of lament for his daughter and her experiences; there is no written record of grief for her lost future. This is ironic as well as tragic, because David is famous for his laments—to this day we read sorrowful words attributed to him in the Psalms. Yet his capacity to lament did not extend to Tamar.

As the head of the family in that culture, David should have been the one to ensure that his son Amnon's actions had consequences. After all, Amnon deceived the king himself and used him to get access to Tamar. But King David did not use his power to bring justice. This sets the stage for his other son Absalom's actions, which we will turn to tomorrow.

When Tamar tells her story, it does not fix the situation. But she claims her dignity and self-worth with her public lament: "This happened to me; I have been wronged."

Churches are places where people go to engage in rituals of lament, at least about some things. When someone dies, we hold funerals, and we expect people to cry and sometimes even to wail. But how good are we at helping people lament other losses?

I knew a woman whose father sexually abused her in her childhood. As an adult, she sought to address this deep pain and shared the process with her church congregation. Months of lament turned into years, and the woman picked up subtle hints from the congregation that she should be getting past her childhood sexual abuse. They asked her not to talk about it anymore in sharing time. A few people suggested she might be "holding on to her pain." Even though the abuse took place during most of her childhood, some congregants expected her to get over it in a year or two. Her healing journey was not as quick and tidy as others wanted it to be.

Most churches are uncomfortable with the rage that many survivors feel and express. Some may suggest that it's not Christian to be so angry. But these feelings and expressions are a natural part of lament. We see these emotions in the Bible, and some writers even call down God's wrath on their oppressors.

Like Tamar, people can live their whole lives suffering the consequences of other people's harmful actions. Children are estranged from their parents, best friends never speak to each other again, communities are divided by racism, and nations become mortal enemies. Jesus came to save us in the midst of tragedies like these. Jesus has the power to heal our pain.

The Nazi regime murdered six million people in death camps, mostly Jews, but also Roma people, priests, people with disabilities, queer people, and political prisoners. For many survivors and their families today, their great sorrow is that huge branches of their family tree were lopped off, their bodies incinerated in ovens or buried in unmarked graves.

A few years ago, I added the micro habit of lament to my day. Micro habits are small, repeated actions that can change us in profound ways. I started following the Auschwitz-Birkenau Memorial and Museum on social media, and each day they show a photo of someone who was in the concentration camp: a seventy-five-year-old, a thirty-five-year-old, a seventeen-year-old, a toddler.[6] Each day I offer a micro lament in response, "Oh no, this life too was snuffed out." When I see the baby's face, I think, "This woman would be seventy-six today; she should be looking back at her life and accomplishments, surrounded by family and friends." I can't comprehend the enormity of six million people murdered, but I'm trying. Even if I continue this micro lament for twenty-five years, I will see the faces of just over nine thousand people (far short of six million); even so, it's a tiny gesture of solidarity.

Forgetting the harm done to others is dangerous. On social media and in the news, I see writers scapegoating "Jewish elites" for world problems. Jewish cemeteries and synagogues are defaced regularly, and Jewish people are targeted with racial slurs and even physical violence.[7] We must not forget the danger of anti-Semitism and where it leads.

Are you able to lament the harm you have experienced? Do you know someone who is lamenting a wrong done to them? If you know of a group of people who are lamenting violence against them, have you taken the time to listen to their pain, to sit with them in their tears, and to compassionately imagine the sorrow their life contains?

> **PRAY:** *God, there are chasms of pain hard to express,*
> *and harder to comprehend.*
> *Our own grief can be like a heavy rock we carry inside us.*
> *Thank you that the horizon of your love*
> *encompasses all of us, and all our emotions.*
> *Help us sojourn with the grief-stricken*
> *and those blown about on the storms of rage and anger.*
> *Give us the capacity, the courage, and the compassion*
> *to be with those who have lost hope and lost heart.*
> *The world is so lamentable.*
> *We remember you in the garden of Gethsemane*
> *weeping for your own suffering,*
> *and for the sin of the world.*
> *We hear your call to join you on our knees. Amen.*

FOR REFLECTION

Do you know someone who has lived their whole life bearing the consequences of someone else's sin? If an example from your own life comes to mind, how has this affected your ability to think about forgiveness?

THURSDAY

Yearning for Restoration

But Absalom spoke to Amnon neither good nor bad, for Absalom hated Amnon because he had raped his sister Tamar. —2 Samuel 13:22

READ: 2 Samuel 13:22–38

This is a Bible story that goes from bad to worse. Absalom is the one person who takes his sister Tamar's pain seriously, but he becomes so consumed with hatred for Amnon that he causes more violence. He intended to care for Tamar by taking her into his house, but instead he orders the murder of Amnon and ends up in exile. Eventually Absalom himself is murdered (2 Samuel 18); no one knows what happened to Tamar after his death.

There are so many horrible, jagged loose ends in this story. There was no repentance from Amnon for what he did. His powerful father ignores Amnon's actions. Revenge destroys more lives. What does Tamar do with her grief and anger about her own rape once Amnon is killed?

When I was a child, our church library had a hardcover book set called *Uncle Arthur's Bedtime Stories*. In each of the short stories, a different child experienced some moral problem, such as little Billy stealing something from the store or little Sally hitting her friend. By the final page of the story, Billy or Sally had confessed their sin and all was forgiven. Each story ended neatly, like a package with a pretty bow on it. I loved reading those stories because they were so orderly and predictable.

But life is not like that. It's terribly messy, and our stories are unruly and often unpredictable. I am glad that the Bible is not like *Uncle Arthur's Bedtime Stories*. If the Bible only contained simple stories, where would we find ourselves?

My father died when I was sixteen, and I was heartbroken because he was the most important person in my life. I was in my late twenties when I found out that he had been violent toward my mother and stepmother. Most of the abuse happened late at night when I was asleep. But when someone told me about it, a memory came flooding back of being in bed in the dark while listening to a fight, and my stepmother's intense cry, "Don't you dare hit me again!"

I felt terribly betrayed and let down by my father. I was filled with anger. This knowledge of his abusive actions colored my once-happy family memories. I couldn't stand to have his picture on my shelf anymore. For a long time I tried not to think about him. Then I went through a period where I had long, one-sided conversations with him in my head. "How could you do this?" I wondered. What other important things did I not know about my father?

It's hard to live with unfinished business—no repentance, no apologies, and no explanations from the wrongdoer, only unresolved grief. *Uncle Arthur's Bedtime Stories* did not prepare me for this reality. Neither did the Bible stories I'd been taught in Sunday school. I had never been exposed to stories like Tamar's. My teachers focused on the happy-ending stories where good conquers evil, such as where the shepherd David kills Goliath, the former prisoner Joseph thrives in Egypt, and the enslaved Israelites are rescued. These stories did not equip me to handle the ragged endings in my own life.

Have you ever had to carry a heavy package for a long distance? You hold it in one arm first, then the other arm; you try carrying it on your shoulder and on your back. Eventually every part of you is tired. Carrying this story about my father felt similar for me. All I wanted was to put it down, but I didn't know how. It felt like it was chained to me with giant iron locks.

Perhaps there are messy stories like this in your life, unfinished business that haunts you. Maybe someone who hurt you has died. Or maybe they are walking around and seem oblivious to the pain they caused you. Are you having conversations with someone in your head in the wee hours of the night? Maybe this is not your reality, but you probably know someone who is experiencing an ongoing, messy story.

It's complicated trying to find peace in this situation. I've prayed about it. I've studied about forgiveness. I've talked to people who knew my dad and tried to understand what was going on in his life. The burden isn't gone completely. I think I've let go of the intensity of the grief, but I doubt I will ever be rid of the deep disappointment. I expected better from him.

There were jagged endings in Jesus' earthly life as well. He didn't want to be crucified or betrayed by people he had discipled. His earthly life was ended when he was just a young man. As the oldest son, he was responsible for his mother, and he had to turn that over to someone else, which must have felt as bitter a prospect as the vinegar he was offered (John 19:26–29).

In the African American spiritual "There Is a Balm in Gilead," the lyrics speak of God making "the wounded whole." God's horizon extends beyond the grave. In this world, we live in the tension of God's reign, which is here, but not fully here. We feel the weight of our woundedness. It's not a comfortable place to be. We do yearn for restoration. Can we trust that resurrection Sunday is coming?

> **PRAY:** *Today we pray for ourselves*
> *and for anyone who is struggling*
> *with burdens that are hard to carry.*

How long, O Lord?
Mother of us all, where is your relief?
When we are stuck, spinning our wheels
    in deep grooves of grief, God, be with us.
When we are incandescent with rage,
        lighting up the night sky above our beds
        with righteous reproaches, God, be with us.
When we hold our heavy heads in our hands,
        too tired to face another day
        with all this heartache, God, be with us.
When we twist and turn,
        trying every conceivable way
        to live with terrible memories, God, be with us.
Give us the gift of imagination,
        and the vision of an unburdened life:
        your salvation that arrives in time.

FOR REFLECTION

In your family, are there jagged endings to stories where no apologies were said and pain lingers? What situations make you yearn for restoration? How is God walking with you in that experience?

Naming Sin

But woe to you Pharisees! For you tithe mint and rue and herbs of all kinds and neglect justice and the love of God; it is these you ought to have practiced, without neglecting the others. —Luke 11:42

READ: Luke 11:37–54

In the Christian tradition, Lent is traditionally a time for self-examination, a time for us to take inventory of our consciences and name the sins we've committed.

Historically, my own Mennonite denomination has been overly focused on sin. Over the centuries, our churches splintered again and again because we could not agree about what was sinful and what was not. We couldn't tolerate going to church with people who sinned in certain ways. We even split churches over what type of hats Christians should wear! There was a surplus of judgment and a deficit of grace.

I see a tendency to overcompensate for these missteps today. Because of this previous unhealthy preoccupation with sin, now we often avoid talking about sin. We just want to be positive and not dwell on the negatives. We may privately think that someone should not have been unfaithful to their marriage vows, or that buying such an expensive car was wasteful, or that a parent could behave more gently with their children. But in church we smile at one another and nod and don't talk about sinful behavior.

Or maybe we know we should talk about sin because the Bible talks about it, but because the topic is uncomfortable for us, we become laser-focused on addressing one type of sin that we haven't committed. We name certain sexual orientations as sinful, or elevate supporting certain political positions as the only "faithful" choice. We become obsessed about protecting sexual purity in the church while ignoring sins like conspicuous consumption, pride, and racism.

How do we talk about sin more faithfully? The Hebrew Bible reveals a God who pursues human beings when we go the wrong way. God gave the law on Mount Sinai to help guide the Israelites, and sent prophets to show them where they were missing the mark. Jesus came to demonstrate God's desire to save us from our sins. He gave his life to demonstrate God's love for us so we would turn and repent.

In Luke 11, Jesus delivers an especially strong call to repentance for religious leaders who focus on small things and neglect justice and love. These words do not express dismissal or hatred of the Pharisees. Jesus talked to Pharisees and ate at their homes. These were his people: they were all Jews worshiping the same God. And precisely because he cared for them, he called out what was happening in his community. He pointed out their greed and pride and their neglect of justice.

I can imagine the wide eyes of some who were listening to this conversation. Suddenly the poor who were overtaxed and overburdened have a champion, someone in their corner. Naming sin as sin is helpful both for the sinned against and the sinners, who are called to repentance.

When someone hurts you terribly, it's as if an insurmountable wall rises between you and that person. Occasionally a person can miraculously leap over such a big wall, but for most of us, there is a lot of hard slogging required to get over the wall. We need to talk about the sin in order to scale the wall.

Making an apology is one way that we name sin. Expressing remorse is not the only thing we need to do to address the problem, but it is an important first step. We learn from childhood that apologies are important. After insulting my sister at the dinner table, I was instructed by my father, "Carol, your words hurt your sister's feelings; you should go and say sorry to her." Learning how to apologize is an important skill parents want children to learn. So many conflicts could be avoided if people had the humility needed to apologize, and the skills to apologize effectively.

As a pastor, I have heard about too many bad apologies. An adult, abused by their mother during childhood, goes to their mother to talk about it. The mother says, "I'm sorry if abuse happened; I'm sorry if you were hurt." This attempt at an apology subtly deflects responsibility from the mother; the *if* casts doubt on whether the abuse even happened. Abuse doesn't just happen. To talk about it as if it fell from the sky and hit someone avoids the fact that one person chose to harm another. Saying "*if* you were hurt" is blaming the victim, because it implies that the person chose to be hurt and could have avoided it.

Instead, good apologies are like stairs to help people climb over the walls we built with our sinful actions. A good apology shows the repentant sinner taking responsibility for wrong actions and not blaming the victim: "I am sorry that I hit you when you were little. It was terrifying for you, and it was all my fault. No child should be hit like that. I knew better and I made bad choices. I deeply regret my actions."

If you think back to a time when you were badly hurt by someone, did you ever receive an apology? Was it a good apology or did you feel blamed for your hurt? Tragically, apologies are often inadequate or not forthcoming at all. What happens then—are we doomed to live alongside that insurmountable wall alone?

Community can play an important role in helping to scale the wall, especially when the person who harmed someone is unrepentant or has died. I have seen churches step into that void and acknowledge the sin and hurt. The church community erects stairs over the wall in place of the one who committed the wrong.

When abuse happens in the church, congregations should apologize to victims. They name the harm that was done: "This abuse was wrong and should not have happened here." The church must go through a process of self-examination, asking, "Are there things we should have done differently? How can we prevent this from happening again?"

All this discussion of apologies and stairs assumes that we can name and talk about sin. If we avoid talking about sin because it's unpleasant, we are ironically committing the sin of omission: not doing something we should. We should pray for insight into our own sins, and cultivate the skill of apologizing. Like Jesus did with the Pharisees, we should be willing to address the sin of others.

PRAY: *Cultivate in us the ability to apologize.*
Give us insight into the error of our ways
*   and give us courage to take responsibility.*
If we are waiting for an apology, give us patience.
Help us create communities that address sin
*   thoroughly, lovingly, wholistically,*
*   in the name of Jesus. Amen.*

FOR REFLECTION

How do you react to the word *sin*? In your faith community, is sin talked about regularly, or only rarely? Has a certain sin created a wall in your relationships or community?

SATURDAY

Confessing Together

If we say that we have fellowship with him while we are walking in darkness, we lie and do not do what is true. —1 John 1:6

READ: 1 John 1:5–10

Walking in the pitch dark is a risk to life and limb. I worked as a camp counselor when I was a young adult. One night a few of the staff with no responsibilities stayed up late, but when it came time to go back to our tents, it was so dark we could not even see our hands in front of our faces. No one had a flashlight (this was the time before cell phones). The camp was in a remote area, so there was no ambient light, and thick clouds obscured the stars and moon. It was so scary groping our way inch by inch through the woods, squinting and seeing nothing. It was a miracle our eyes weren't poked out by branches or that we didn't trip and break a limb.

I resonate with the imagery of 1 John 1. What if that night in the camp we had acted as if we could see perfectly? Denial of the surrounding darkness would have meant we charged ahead to certain injury. We need the light in order to move ahead safely. Publicly renouncing the things of darkness is important because we are all very likely to stumble in the dark.

Years ago I saw that my neighbor's ten-year-old had a large, dark blue bruise on his leg. I asked whether he got it playing soccer, and he said, "My dad kicked me because I wouldn't get off the couch." I told him I was sorry this happened and that his dad should not have treated him like that. I thought of reporting it to our local child protection agency, but I was intimidated by my unfriendly neighbor, who practiced martial arts in his backyard and had a big, mean dog. I rationalized that this boy's mother should report that bruise.

I had no idea when I made that choice how it would eventually fill me with regret. How for the rest of my life, to this day, I would wonder what happened to that boy and whether he told anyone else about the violence. I sinned by not speaking up and helping that boy. I put my own fears of awkward conflict with a neighbor over the safety of a vulnerable child.

It's hard to confess this sin. I hate to think that others might think me a callous person because I ignored the pain of a child. But that is exactly what I did. And to make it more inexplicable, I was a mother with children at home at the time. If I had seen the bruise on my child, I would have been up in arms, but I could not find enough compassion in my heart for the neighbor boy to do something. I am mortified thinking about it now.

The middle-class, white Canadian culture I grew up in valued the nuclear family and its privacy. What happened at home, stayed at home. Growing up, no one outside my family knew about the violence within it. That's the way things were. I think this deeply internalized belief influenced my response to the violence occurring in my neighbor's house. It doesn't excuse it, but it helps me understand it. Like Cain in Genesis 4:9, I wondered, "Am I my brother's keeper?" Like Cain, I didn't think I was.

The Holy Spirit comes as a light in our lives, illuminating our sinfulness and calling us to repentance. When I learned more about child abuse, I came to see the light. I am clearer now about my responsibilities to report child abuse going forward.

My friend Lydia Neufeld-Harder recently wrote about her own journey of repentance in an article coauthored by her daughter Ingrid Bettina Wolfear. Lydia and her husband, Gary Harder, adopted Ingrid, an Indigenous child, when she was a toddler. Their church conference was encouraging people to adopt Indigenous children. As a white family, they thought that all they had to do was love Ingrid, and everything would be fine.

While there was love in abundance, they were entirely unprepared for the challenges their daughter would face as an Indigenous person in a white family in a white community. Ingrid's path was filled with identity struggles and pain from racist remarks and actions.

It was only decades later that Lydia and Gary began to grasp the racist agenda of the Canadian government that removed a whole generation of Indigenous children from their parents and families. (Though this systematic practice began in the 1950s and extended into the 1980s, it is referred to as the Sixties Scoop.) Ingrid was not an orphan. She had been stolen from her mother and her community as they tried to cope with trauma inflicted on them from their time in residential schools.

These two stories—of the neighbor's child and me, and of Lydia, Gary, and Ingrid—illustrate that sometimes repentance is not simply saying, "I did the wrong thing." Sometimes repentance means trying to unpack the complex layers of why we thought and acted the way we did. Whole communities need to confess and engage in this process. We are often unwittingly part of interlocking systems that perpetuate abuse and hatred.

It is not easy to talk about my failure to protect that child, but I share it as a reminder of our collective responsibility to protect children. We need to support each other to take risks and speak up when we think a child is not safe.

Lydia and Ingrid have spoken out about their family's experience to encourage us all to examine our collective sinfulness. Lydia's individual choices happened in the context of a church and a society that were racist and treated Indigenous families without respect or compassion. She tells her story to remind people that good intentions are not enough. We need to be wise enough to look beyond the surface of sin and humble enough to confess together.

> **PRAY:** *God, we need your help*
> *when we are obstinately oblivious*
> *to larger patterns of sin in our lives.*
> *Collective sin is so complicated,*
> *we are tempted to throw up our hands,*
> *or just put our heads down*
> *and try not to think about it.*
> *But you provide illumination.*
> *You will help us find ways to address systemic sin,*
> *and you will give us companions to do it with. Thank you.*

FOR REFLECTION

Think about the state or country you live in currently. Is there a system you can think of that leads individuals into temptation and sin? What do we miss if we only focus on individual sin? Can you think of ways you might address that larger system to effect change?

SUNDAY

Calling for Repentance

Then Peter remembered what Jesus had said: "Before the cock crows, you will deny me three times." And he went out and wept bitterly. —Matthew 26:75

READ: Matthew 26:69–75

That night by the fire, Peter may have had numerous reasons for not admitting he was a follower of Jesus. Maybe he thought he would be sent away if they found out he was a disciple of the arrested man. Peter told Jesus he would never forsake him, so he was determined to stay close. If it took a little fib to make that happen, Peter was willing to risk it.

The people around the fire weren't satisfied. They pressed Peter again, so he had to lie a second time. And then a third time he says, "I do not know that man." A spotlight suddenly illuminates his actions when he hears the cock crow. Peter remembers Jesus' warning that he would deny him three times. Peter is convicted of his sin and weeps bitterly.

When someone points out a sin I am committing, I often get annoyed or defensive. But if I am open to listening and willing to be honest with myself, the call to repentance is an amazing opportunity to change before things get worse.

As a pastor, I have thought deeply about pastoral care and the importance of calling people to repentance. In our worship services, this can happen through congregational prayers.

I regularly teach a class on worship where I ask students to write a congregational prayer that will include a specific call to repentance, such as:

"For all who could have been generous this week but hoarded their money for themselves, hear our prayer."

"For times we have looked down on someone because of the color of their skin, forgive us."

"Help us see how things we are addicted to are destroying our lives and relationships."

Honest prayers are important because the Holy Spirit can use them to touch our hearts. There is a fine line between a prayer that pinpoints and illuminates our sin and a prayer that shames and overwhelms us with too much negativity. I have heard students list so many sins in one prayer that my mind shuts down. Worship leaders need to seek God's guidance as they think about how to pray publicly.

Many churches have lay worship leaders who volunteer to lead worship. Each Sunday, different people pray publicly, and so hopefully a wide variety of concerns is addressed in prayer. But my observation of this practice is that most worship leaders don't want to mention sin. They are happy to share things the congregation is thankful for, but as volunteers, worship leaders are not sure they have the authority to say hard things, like a call to repentance. If worship leaders just skim the surface and hardly mention sin, who will encourage us to repent?

Since violence in the family is just as much a reality in Christian homes as in secular homes, I encourage my students to mention this in their prayers: "Help us see how the words we speak have wounded those we love. Help us apologize thoroughly and mean it."

"We pray for those here who have been violent in word or deed toward their family members. Help them admit they have a problem and reach out for help."

"For all who feel unsafe as they lay down to sleep in their homes because of family violence, hear our prayer. God, help us address actions that make our families feel unsafe."

In the past year, what prayers have you heard in your congregation? Have your worship leaders specifically named abuse, greed, racism, prejudice, or pride as something your congregation needs to confess? Are these sins that we are hesitant to name in our own prayers?

Praying about sin is not just about caring for people in the congregation. It's about mission and outreach as well. When newcomers visit the church, they listen to what we say in our prayers. They are curious about the community. If we only acknowledge positive things publicly, we can come across as a community that is pretending to be good and hiding what has gone wrong. Honesty in the church can be invitational to newcomers because it teaches that God welcomes sinners here.

A congregation I am familiar with was going through a difficult conflict, since some people in the church wanted to fully include LGBTQ+ people as pastors, and others did not. After a long period of discernment, the church held a vote, and they decided to exclude LGBTQ+ people from ministry. This was a difficult decision that left many people heartbroken. In Sunday morning worship the week after the vote, the pastor offered a lengthy prayer of confession that named the pain and hurt in the church. The pastor was dismayed when some first-time visitors attended church that Sunday because the emotions of regular attendees were so raw. But those newcomers decided they wanted to join the church. They were attracted to a congregation that could be open about conflict and not hide it.

Calling people to repentance is not for the faint of heart. It takes courage to name sin out loud. Think of the prophets who went to the people of Israel and delivered unpopular messages to powerful people. They were often threatened with death or chased away. But

God sent them with a specific message and for a purpose and they followed through.

We are all loved by God, but people who are loved by God still do very bad things. During this season of Lent, listen carefully for how God might be calling you to repentance through prayers and prophets.

PRAY: *You are the God who sees us.*
You see where we do right, and where we do wrong.
Thank you for sending the Holy Spirit,
    who gives us course corrections.
Even though we can be cranky
    and we don't want to listen,
    thank you for caring enough
    to call us to repentance
    and to set us on paths where we can make right
    the wrongs we've done. Amen.

FOR REFLECTION

Consider a time when you were called to repentance. Was it through a prayer, a sermon, a conversation with someone, or simply an inner conviction? Do you think your congregation does a good job calling people to repentance? Why or why not?

MONDAY

Relieving Shame

Cain said to the LORD, "My punishment is greater than I can bear!"
—Genesis 4:13

READ: Genesis 4:8–16

Cain committed premeditated murder, yet it seems to have come as a huge shock to him that his life would be changed by murdering his brother.

When I was a grade four student, my classmates and I were given little boxes so we could collect pennies and nickels for the United Nations Children's Fund when we went trick-or-treating on Halloween. I did this dutifully, but I kept forgetting to return the box. Eventually, the teacher stopped reminding us to return the boxes. So, I opened my box and used the money to buy myself potato chips. The chips tasted good, but I had long-term mental indigestion that year from realizing that I was the type of person who would steal from starving children.

As an adult, I went on a learning tour to Kenya. When we approached a border crossing, the tour guide warned us not to give out money to beggars. A Maasai woman, holding a very tiny baby, came up to me holding out her hand. The baby did not look very healthy. I thought about giving her something, but I didn't because the tour guide told us we shouldn't. I felt bad for her, and I felt bad that I could not help her.

The following year I had a baby of my own, and suddenly that woman wasn't just a beggar—in my mind and in my heart, I understood that she was a mother trying to feed her child. As I fed my own baby I was haunted by the woman's face. It would have been no hardship for me to share some of the money I was carrying that day, but I didn't want to risk displeasing the tour guide. Now I wished I would have risked something to be generous.

These experiences have remained with me. When I am tempted to do bad things or remain inactive instead of doing good things, I wonder, Do I want to live with this memory?

John Witmer was a conscientious objector to military service in World War I. Raised in a pacifist community of Ohio Mennonites, he believed that killing people was wrong. He was conscripted and forced into a military camp. While John was there he was mercilessly persecuted, and other recruits nearly killed him several times. He became sick with influenza, and in the middle of the night, a group of soldiers threw him in the shower, soaking him with cold water. He had no warm clothes or blankets to shield him from the subzero temperatures in the unheated barracks. He died of his illness three days later. John's body was sent home to his grieving family.

In the 1960s, around forty years later, an older man appeared in the community where John Witmer was born, looking for his relatives. People directed him to the home of Ida, John's youngest sister. The man explained he had been one of the men who had thrown her brother in the cold shower when he was sick. Ever since that day, he had regretted what he had done. He told Ida he was coming now to say sorry to the family for his role in John's death. He came to ask for forgiveness.

Ida offered words of forgiveness. She was thankful that this man was taking responsibility for his unkind actions, and that he had lived to repent of them. It gave her and her family a certain closure to learn that a person who had persecuted John had ultimately regretted his actions.

What was done to John was only one of many millions of acts of violence in World War I. People who participate in wars or who are victimized by war carry so many stories of atrocities. They often experience post-traumatic stress for what was done to them or guilt for the inhumanity they displayed to other human beings.

In church communities, we might never know the shame and guilt that some people carry. I once worked in a church where the previous pastor had also led a prison ministry. Several people who served their time were released and started attending our church. There is a lot of discrimination against people who were formerly incarcerated, but it is especially directed at those who have committed sexual crimes against children.

In that congregation, I learned how hurtful terms like *predator*, *pedophile*, and *child molester* can be. We do not regularly refer to people in church by the sins they have committed. I don't call my congregants liars, cheaters, bullies, or gluttons. We are always more than the sins we commit. Because of the formerly incarcerated people who attended my church, I learned about the burden of shame carried by people who have hurt children; they will carry it for their whole lives. The challenge upon leaving prison is to forge a new identity and to find the strength to not re-offend. This delicate process is not aided by being labeled and continually told that you are the sin you committed.

I am not advocating for crimes like child sexual abuse to be forgotten or for children to be put in danger through exposure to people who are struggling not to re-offend. On the contrary, in that church we put important protections in place around people who had offended so they would not be placed in temptation's way. We didn't forget, but we also didn't label. We offered the hope of a better future for them with God's help, and the help of counselors and parole officers.

When we commit sins, we hurt others—yes. But we also hurt ourselves, because our own life stories will be shaped negatively by these actions. With the help of the Holy Spirit, we can relieve our shame and resist piling shame on others.

PRAY: *We have sinned.*
God, sometimes the burden of shame crushes us;
  our regret and remorse
  can feel like too much to bear.
We wonder what kind of people we are.
Thank you for showing us
  that we are your kind of people.
With your help, we have a future where we can make
  different, better, and healthier choices. Amen.

FOR REFLECTION

What have you learned from thinking about the sins you've committed? Has anticipating guilt or shame kept you from committing a sin? During this season of Lent, are you being called to offer an apology to someone? What holds you back from offering it? Have you ever been labelled by someone because of a sin you committed? How did that feel?

TUESDAY

Encountering Walls

The dead man came out, his hands and feet bound with strips of cloth and his face wrapped in a cloth. Jesus said to them, "Unbind him, and let him go." —John 11:44

READ: John 11:1–45

Raising Lazarus from the dead was one of the most shocking miracles that Jesus performed. The sight of Lazarus returning into the land of the living was surely something no one present would ever forget. This miracle is also a parable, a lesson to remind us that even when we are dead in sin, enslaved to sinful ways, Jesus can reach in and bring us to life. Jesus frees us from death.

Over the past decade, I've been reading more about polarization in both the United States and Canada. There are sharp differences on so many issues, including politics, economics, and race. We think that we are right and other groups are wrong. That itself is not a problem, since disagreement and conflict are as old as civilization; we will never completely agree with one another. But we plunge into the dangerous water of polarization when we think there is no point in talking anymore and that dialogue is fruitless. Extreme polarization leads to thinking of the person who disagrees with us, or the group they are a part of, as less than human. When we dehumanize people, it opens the door for violence.

During the COVID-19 pandemic, people in my circle of friends supported different positions about the disease, with some friends questioning whether there even was a pandemic. I found it hard to talk when we were so diametrically opposed. I would gossip about these people with whom I disagreed. At first it seemed exciting to talk about "us" and "them." I felt energized. Walls between us kept growing. But in time I became uncomfortable with how reluctant I felt to talk to certain people, thinking, "There's no point." For me, a small breakthrough came when one of my "opponents" became a mom and I was able to bring something over for the baby. This small human gesture reminded me, "Hey, these are people—not the enemy."

We see the deadly consequences of this dehumanizing mindset wherever racism flourishes. In 2023 in Kansas City, Missouri, sixteen-year-old Ralph Yarl was shot twice by a white homeowner, Andrew Lester, simply for ringing his doorbell. Yarl, who is Black, was picking up his brothers from a playdate and had accidentally gone to the wrong door. Lester shot Yarl twice through the closed door. Yarl survived but lives with a brain injury. This is only one example of so many incidents where white people have behaved aggressively toward Black people. In some cases, Black people have been murdered, and those who killed them have often faced few consequences.[8] When we dehumanize another group, we see them as a threat that needs to be eliminated.

Of course, thinking of people as less than human is an unchristian attitude. God made all of us, and loves all of us. Jesus came to save everyone, and no one is beyond God's care. Dehumanizing others builds walls of division that God never intended.

How do we break down these walls between people? Antiracism efforts help to address racial tension. In Canada and South Africa, Truth and Reconciliation processes have helped in some ways, but they have not been entirely successful.

When walls are built because of crimes like theft, Victim Offender Reconciliation programs can help. A homeowner who is robbed, for example, often assumes the worst about the person who stole things. They might imagine a hardened criminal who poses a threat to their personal safety, and they subsequently don't feel safe in their own home anymore. On the other side, the person who stole may assume that the homeowner has insurance and is so wealthy that they may hardly notice what is missing.

When victims and offenders talk together with the help of a trained mediator, they can come to realize that they are both people with feelings. As both parties hear about the motivation for the crime and the impact of the crime, it opens space for the possibility of an apology, restitution, and forgiveness.

It is tempting to place all evil on the "other." We assign evil to a cultural or racial group, or we demonize and bemoan refugees, or people who are undocumented, or people who live below—or far above—the poverty line. The Russian writer Aleksandr Solzhenitsyn challenged exactly this attitude when he wrote, "The line between good and evil passes . . . right through every human heart."[9]

A friend of mine recently immigrated to Canada from Ukraine, fleeing the war there. She was in the city of Mariupol when it became one of the first cities to be sieged and heavily bombed by invading Russian forces. My friend witnessed firsthand how easily the veneer of civilization is peeled off when people are starving. She observed people being willing to kill each other to get food. These weren't enemies squaring off over food; these were people on the same side of the war, people being invaded. She observed that it is remarkably easy to treat other people as less than human.

The German philosopher Hannah Arendt called this ability to do great wrongs "the banality of evil."[10] Most evil is done not by people with no moral compass, but by everyday good people put in difficult circumstances. We are all capable of building dividing walls.

PRAY: *God, so often we claim you for our side,*
and think that you cannot possibly care
for people who disagree with us.

Your love calls us to a new place,
 to step with faith beyond this world of polarizing sides.
You lead us to an inside-out world,
 where our enemy is our sibling,
 where our foe can be our fondest friend.
You call us to be firm believers
 in the one who crossed heaven and earth
 to show that even between God and human beings
 there are no sides.
It is in the name of Jesus Christ,
 whose arms embrace us all,
 that we pray today. Amen.

FOR REFLECTION

Have you witnessed polarization in your community? Perhaps people are taking hardened stances regarding the issues of gun safety and ownership, equitable access to health insurance, or abortion. How might God be calling you to reach out in compassion across a wall?

PURSUING

FREEDOM

WEDNESDAY

Turning to God

So it is not the will of your Father in heaven that one of these little ones should be lost. —Matthew 18:14

READ: Matthew 18:12–14

Some of the most famous verses in the Bible about forgiveness are found in Matthew 18. There is a lot to learn from one chapter, so we will unpack it gradually in the coming days. It's funny that in a scripture passage that talks about finding things that are lost, verse 11 itself is missing from the main text; it appears as a footnote. Verse and chapter numbers were added to the Bible in the 1500s. Since then, earlier manuscripts of the Bible have been discovered that don't contain the phrase found in the footnoted verse 11, so biblical scholars have determined it was a later addition. You can imagine an ancient monk copying out the gospel of Matthew, wanting to make the point more emphatically than the original gospel writer did with the now-footnoted point: "For the Son of Man came to save the lost."

Sometimes we find ourselves lost in bewildering ways. We don't set out to become mired in harmful practices, but we find ourselves drawn in anyway. Here's an example. The casual drinker, who likes to have a glass of wine at night, decides after a stressful day that maybe drinking two glasses would be better to take the edge off. Circumstances grow worse, and the amount of drinking increases to match.

Fast-forward, and there is a dawning realization that so much has been sacrificed for the drinking—family relationships are strained, employment is terminated, and friends abandoned. There was no signpost at the beginning of this road advertising "This way to despair," but that is where it leads. We can feel lost and alone but God never loses track of us.

A student once shared with me how God found her when she was mired in addiction to crack cocaine. Her whole life revolved around where to get the drug and, once she had it, how to get more. Her life was going from bad to worse, and her relationships with her family had been shattered. In a downtown shop window she saw the words "Jesus saves." She said it was as if the words were glowing, as if they were a specific message from God to her. That night she turned to Jesus and asked him to save her. God was able to free her from her addiction, and she began the long process of trying to heal her broken human relationships as well.

When we find ourselves in trouble, not knowing which way to turn, we can pray. God is like a divine GPS (global positioning system). God always knows how to get us from here (sin central) to a better place (grace). There are no closed roads in the directions God gives us. God will talk us through every turn, reminding us to stay in the right lane.

When we consider the impact of a sin we have committed, we can get that terrible sinking feeling in our stomach. If we turn to God to ask for help, God will meet us at our lowest place. When we understand that God forgives us, the love of God floods through us. There is a word for that state of being made whole: *absolution*. In some church denominations, absolution is administered by priests in a formal way, but the term names the universal Christian experience of being forgiven by God.

Feeling found when we are lost and feeling released from guilt is an amazing spiritual experience. That is Day One. Day Two, we have to start that repentance journey, where we show our penitence by acting in new ways, with new patterns of behavior.

Victims of sin can also feel lost. When we are hurt, betrayed, or violated, it can feel like the home we've always known has burned to the ground. We don't know where to turn with our pain. Jesus also pursues those who are lost through no fault of their own. God is the loving shepherd who will not sleep till the lamb is found.

When a child is abused by a parent or caregiver, this causes terrible confusion. The person that child loves, on whom they rely, is also the person who hurts them. This is a deeply conflictual situation for children. Child abuse can have a devastating effect on a child's beliefs, development, self-esteem, and ability to function.

Survivors of abuse, including child abuse, often blame themselves. They may feel they did something to deserve the abuse. A friend who was sexually abused by a neighbor as a very young girl told me that she felt that she was responsible. Every time the person abused her, they gave her a nickel. She wanted the nickel, and she took it each time. And so she felt that she was agreeing to the abuse, as if it were some sort of transaction. It took intensive therapy for her to accept and believe it was not her fault.

Or child abuse survivors may worry that something is wrong with them, that they are dirty, or intrinsically bad. People who experience childhood abuse often lose a sense of self as good and worthy of love.

I recently read a memoir about the process of healing from child sexual abuse. The author, Pamela Frey, shares how her therapist helped her befriend her younger, six-year-old self. Little Pamela was abused by an uncle, she was lost and alone, and she didn't know whom she could trust. Adult Pamela imagined going back in time and embracing little Pamela, assuring her that she was lovable and good. She titled her memoir *The Woman Who Picked Up Her Child: Creative, Transformative Healing from Childhood Sexual Abuse.*

Lost does not have to be a permanent condition. Jesus is seeking us. Do we want to turn to God and be found?

PRAY: *God, you are the Wayfinder.*
When we are impossibly lost
    in mazes of our own making,
    or adrift because someone hijacked us,
    you search us out, calling us by name.
No one is beyond recovery.
With you by our side,
    we see a different future rising,
    hopeful on the horizon's edge. Amen.

FOR REFLECTION

Do you know someone who experienced a sense of being lost after a grievous sin? Have you ever experienced the feeling of being lost? Did your community reach out to you?

THURSDAY

Finding Deliverance

Indeed, I know their sufferings, and I have come down to deliver them from the Egyptians. —Exodus 3:7–8

READ: Exodus 3:1–12

God delivers us from evil. This good news permeates both the Hebrew Bible and the New Testament. God loves us, knows when we are in danger, and wants to save us. Churches live out this good news by helping people who are seeking deliverance from oppression. Many churches have sponsored refugees as they flee violence and persecution.

The congregation I attend has been doing this work since the 1970s. Over the decades we have partnered with government programs to sponsor families from Laos, Bosnia, Colombia, Congo, Syria, and Afghanistan. Each family carries a story of loss, violence, and fear. We welcome them to Canada, providing shelter, friendship, and a helping hand to a new life. We do this in the name of Jesus, who is always in the business of deliverance.

My own grandparents came to Canada in 1923, fleeing violence in Ukraine. My grandmother boarded a train car with her extended family when she was nine months pregnant, and gave birth en route. That little baby (my uncle Andy) and all his brothers grew up in safety because churches in Canada guaranteed the travel loans for this group fleeing oppression.

As my congregation has welcomed refugee newcomers, we too have been delivered—from our own closemindedness. We are learning about different cultures and traditions. Almost everyone in the congregation has had some contact with these families. Many became friends. It's difficult to be hardhearted or prejudiced against newcomers to our country when you look in the eyes of someone telling you a heartbreaking story of forced migration.

The newcomer families have also opened our eyes to the problems in our own country. I've gone with a newcomer to a job interview, and I've seen the interviewer's eyes glaze over in response to hearing the applicant's heavily accented English. I've heard racist and hate-filled comments that neighbors and strangers on the street have said to newcomers. I have been delivered from any pretense that violence and prejudice is just a problem "out there" in other countries—it is alive and well in our own communities.

Churches can also address the flood of refugees in the world by advocating to our governments to give refuge. When we live in a country that is relatively stable, we can be suspicious of countries that experience unrest or war. This sometimes evolves into fear of people from those countries. Perhaps we worry they will bring that unrest here. These fears can be racist too; refugee groups with lighter color skin often receive more help. Churches can challenge these prejudices.

But churches have not always been willing to help people find deliverance. Historically, churches have counseled individuals, especially women, to return to violent or abusive marriage partners. Preserving the marriage has seemed more important than securing the safety of those suffering abuse, including children.

Given the strong biblical message that God delivers us from suffering, you would think that churches would be at the forefront of the domestic violence shelter movement. Sadly, workers at such shelters are often suspicious of pastors and churches who have too often tried to pressure people to return to "save their marriage."

Here's an example. A woman flees to a shelter for people suffering from domestic violence. The husband who has abused her goes to their pastor and vows he is sorry and wants to change. He complains that his wife won't forgive him even though he has apologized. The husband, who just wants to gain control of his wife once again, manipulates the pastor to intervene. The pastor uses their spiritual authority to persuade the wife to return. The good behavior of the husband lasts for a short time, and the cycle of violence begins again. People who are abusive can't stop abusing with a quick prayer. There are deep issues that need to be addressed in counseling, and it's important that safety be prioritized over people remaining in the same home to preserve a marriage.

When I pastored, one of the elderly women in my church shared with me that her husband was screaming at her, grabbing her by the hair, and shoving her against the wall. His violence was escalating. I told her that God did not want her to live in fear and that her husband needed help. She deserved a safe place to live. But she was determined not to leave him, saying, "I made a vow to stay with him." Some weeks later, she agreed to go to a shelter just to talk to a counselor. The workers at the shelter were worried for her life because her husband had a gun and had isolated her by removing the house phone and forbidding her from having a cell phone. She was unable to call for help from her rural home. Still, she felt it was her duty to stay with her husband.

In this case, it was not me as the representative of her church who was encouraging her to stay in a dangerous place; it was the theology she inherited from the time she was a little girl. "Marriage is forever," she had been taught, "and a good wife never breaks her marriage vow." I was relieved when this woman was delivered, not because she left, but because her husband died from an illness.

God calls us toward forgiveness. People are better able to consider the possibility of forgiveness if they are safe and free from the power of the one who abused them. Interrupting a cycle of abuse by providing safety for an abused person helps the person abusing too. The person who is abusing needs to stop sinning. With time and space to think about abusive actions and the harm caused, there is opportunity for someone who is abusing to seek help and find deliverance as well.

> **PRAY:** *God, you are the Great Deliverer.*
> *For those among us who have struggled*
>   *and waited so long for the promised land*
>   *of freedom and equality,*
>   *we trust in you to help us.*
> *For those who have harmed others,*
>   *and are trapped in cycles of abusing,*
>   *we know that only you can save us.*
> *We stand together on holy ground*
>   *as you deliver us from evil,*
>   *within and without. Amen.*

FOR REFLECTION

Have you seen the church doing the work of deliverance in someone's life? Has your congregation responded to a family experiencing domestic violence? Was the congregation able to help the family end the abusive cycle, or were there things that hindered the family from finding safety or healing?

FRIDAY

Heading for Safety

But he passed through the midst of them and went on his way.
—Luke 4:30

READ: Luke 4:14–30; Mark 3:31–35

Today's story from Luke happens at the very beginning of Jesus' ministry. Jesus has just come down the mountain from his temptation and has begun preaching in Galilee to great success. And then he goes to his hometown of Nazareth.

At first the people in his community thought Jesus spoke well. They admire his gracious words. But then he shares a message that God has and will help people beyond the Jewish tradition. This enrages them, and they drive Jesus out of town to the brow of the hill near Nazareth, intending to throw him off the cliff.

I have been to Nazareth and climbed the hills around it. They are very large and steep and not something you scramble up in a minute or two. Your legs become tired, you feel out of breath. I can imagine the crowd murmuring and panting as they drag Jesus up and up. When they reach the summit, something has suddenly changed. Did God intervene to change the hearts of the crowd or provide a protective bubble around Jesus? What we know is that Jesus walks right through them to safety.

Nazareth was not a big place. These were not strangers threatening to kill Jesus. These are people he grew up with: school buddies, neighbors, friends of his parents. It must have been terrifying. What I find noteworthy is not just that Jesus walks through this murderous crowd, but that he walks away from Nazareth permanently. After the crowd of familiar people tries to kill him, he puts distance between himself and them. He never goes back. The Gospels report that he was often called "Jesus of Nazareth," which must have reminded him of this painful story.

I know quite a few people who experienced abuse in their family settings. The ones who are Christians faced enormous pressure from family and their church to forgive the harm done and reconcile with the family members who hurt them. This pressure can come from the offending parties themselves, who minimize their actions and even sometimes demand, "You have to forgive me."

For some abuse survivors I know, freeing themselves from their family was the healthiest and safest option. They cut off communication with people who both hurt them and failed to take responsibility for that hurting.

In my own life, I had a very troubled relationship with my stepmother, who joined our family when I was eight. We had an intense and complicated relationship. I felt manipulated and emotionally abused, particularly during my teenage years when I lived alone with her after my father died and my siblings had left home.

The relationship did not get easier as I aged. People often say, "As you get older you start to appreciate your parents more!" I have found the opposite is also true. As a child, it can be common to make excuses for parents' abusive behavior, wanting desperately to believe that your parents love you, even when all evidence proves the opposite. It's only when you are grown and have developed other supports that you recognize abuse.

At a certain point in my early thirties, I broke off contact with my stepmother for a few years. This was a huge decision for me, and I felt enormously guilty about it. I had recurring nightmares that I had murdered my stepmother and buried her in my backyard! My subconscious was working overtime. Shouldn't good Christian (step)daughters forgive and forget?

My pastor at the time knew my story and the terrible weight I was carrying about this relationship. He reminded me of the story of the bent-over woman (Luke 13:10–17), a woman who had been disabled for eighteen years until Jesus healed her. My pastor said, "This bad relationship has been weighing you down for so long, it could be that Jesus wants to free you from it." His words gave me permission to unburden myself of the guilt that was driving me to meet regularly with someone who was hurting me. I was able to have some much-needed space where I could think more clearly about both what I needed to receive and what I could offer.

The gospels of Mark and Luke both describe Jesus' mother Mary and his brothers and sisters coming to talk to him (Mark 3:31; Luke 8:19). I wonder what they wanted to say. In Jesus' time, family ties were very strong. As an eldest son, Jesus would have been expected to care for his mother. In many parts of the world today, people commonly move away from home to go to school or for job opportunities, or they fall in love with someone who lives at a great distance. We may find it hard to understand the settled nature of the community to which Jesus belonged. For Jesus and his followers, giving up a settled life and traveling from place to place challenged family ties.

When his family draws near, Jesus goes so far as to say, "Who are my mother and my brothers?" (Mark 3:33). He answers his own question: "Whoever does the will of God is my brother and sister and mother" (Mark 3:35). Jesus gives permission to think differently about family. He also creates a community of followers, instructing them to love each other. We often speak of "church family" precisely because of this teaching.

For people who leave abusive families of origin, the church can serve a very important function. In this new church family space, we can feel loved. If church is a secure space, we are more likely to see forgiveness dawning as a possibility on the horizon. Tragically, some people turn to the church as a substitute family and experience judgment and prejudice. If church is a place where we are excluded and judged, where can we turn?

PRAY: *Jesus, you know families from the inside out.*
Hear our prayer for families.
Thank you for families that get along,
*   showing unconditional love and affection.*
We lament that in other families,
*   hostility, put-downs, and violence are the norm.*
Help and strengthen those who will see family this Easter
*   with their shields up and heads tucked down for protection,*
*   not sure if family is a home at all.*
Comfort those who have made a break
*   to prioritize safety.*
Bless those who are working to create
*   new networks of caring and support*
*   in our church families. Amen.*

FOR REFLECTION

Think about a time when you or someone you know was betrayed or desperately hurt by a close friend or family member. What scars resulted from that experience? How did you or the person you know foster safety moving forward? Has setting boundaries with family members been a part of your faith journey?

SATURDAY

Taking Time

Jesus said to him, "Not seven times, but, I tell you, seventy-seven times." —Matthew 18:22

READ: Matthew 18:1–22

Peter probably thought that seven was a generous number of times to forgive someone, so he suggests it to Jesus. But Jesus counters with a huge number as the forgiveness "maximum." Counting up to seventy-seven human interactions is likely unrealistic. I think Jesus is signaling that forgiveness is not about numbers. We need to cultivate an attitude of forgiveness toward each other where we don't count how many times we forgive. When Jesus tells Peter we should forgive seventy-seven times, he is also acknowledging that forgiving is not a one-time act. Dealing with people who sin against us repeatedly is a long process.

In many ways, the call to forgive unceasingly is a good mantra for community life. We hurt each other in many small ways when we work and live together. I love Ephesians 4:32 where it calls us to "be kind to one another, tenderhearted, forgiving one another, as God in Christ has forgiven you." Nursing resentment and anger will never provide a way forward, which is why the writer of Ephesians further encourages us to "be angry but do not sin" (4:26).

Forgiving someone does not mean that we excuse sin or stop talking about it. Jesus continually calls people in power who are hurting others to accept responsibility for their actions. He doesn't say to powerful people, "Don't worry about what you did; I forgive you." No! He holds them to account for the harm they are causing and urges them to make restitution and stop sinning.

How does this approach apply in today's world? Here's an example. You may forgive the business partner who cheated you, leaving you with the bills. However, in three months' time when you have to declare bankruptcy, you may feel another wave of resentment and may choose to forgive your former partner again. Then when your car dies and you can't get a car loan because your credit score is wrecked, the choice to forgive is before you. You will still face the consequences of your business partner's sin.

The same pattern is true for people who break their marriage vows by having sex with someone who is not their partner. In marriage, we generally need to let go of small things, like an occasional unkind remark, and try to have an attitude of forgiveness. But some betrayals in marriage are harder to forgive than others. It takes time to forgive unfaithfulness, and even long periods of time can be insufficient for some people to find a way to forgive and remain married.

A person who has been unfaithful may quickly ask for forgiveness from their partner. But speedy forgiveness does not address the underlying issues, such as why the straying spouse sought out another sexual partner. What is really happening in this marriage? Forgiveness is too often requested and given as a way to avoid a deep and thorough examination of the state of the marital union.

I think of a friend whom I'll call Ana. Her husband was sexually unfaithful numerous times. What does forgiveness look like for her? It did not mean she stayed in the marriage, forgiving seventy-seven times, only to be betrayed over and over again. She found a place of safety when she left the marriage.

As months and years pass, Ana may want to forgive her now ex-husband, but in many ways the harm he did to her continues. She no longer has a partner. She shares custody of their children with him 50/50, which means half of the time, she can't see her children. Their dad has a new, live-in partner, so there is an adult involved in the kids' lives whom she did not choose. Her ex-husband's child support is irregular, so she has many financial worries. And perhaps worst of all, his betrayal means Ana's ability to trust has been corroded, so she can't conceive how she would begin to date anyone again.

Forgiving her ex-husband is something Ana would like to do. As she lives with the consequences of his betrayal every day, she wakes up and makes the decision to walk the road to forgiveness. Instead of thinking of him with hatred, she decides to just let him go. She decides to forgive not once, but seventy times seventy times seven. She makes a fresh decision every day of her life.

But it doesn't mean Ana says, "It's OK; it doesn't matter." Every day it matters. Things are broken for her. She is still so hurt that she can't think of being friends with her ex-husband again. Going to visit him and his lovely young wife in their beautiful home where he is raising a second family is not on her agenda. That will not bring her peace.

Instead, forgiveness means that Ana tries to stop having conversations with him in her head. She hoped to receive a genuine apology for years, a longing which left her continually disappointed. Now, Ana shifts her expectations. She stops putting energy into trying to make him understand her point of view, and moves on.

Forgiveness can mean taking back the emotional power someone has had over you and walking away from any relationship. This type of forgiveness can take years. It can take decades. This type of forgiveness feels very different from forgiveness where someone who hurt you takes full accountability.

Our churches and communities are filled with people on different forgiveness journeys. There are many hurts we carry privately zipped in our knapsacks on the road; no one knows about them. We desperately want to lay those burdens down. We don't want to be forever padlocked to the people who hurt us. We want to be free.

Knowing this, how can our church communities be places where we nurture and sustain each other? Providing loving and supportive environments is essential. Our communities can walk with us on the days we manage to forgive, and on the days when we can't. Our communities can pray for us, and we can wait for God's miracle of forgiveness together.

> **PRAY**: *We are parched pilgrims on a dry, desert journey.*
> *Forgiveness is the water on the horizon,*
> *and we cannot possibly walk there.*
> *We are plagued with hurt—the betrayal, the verbal barbs,*
> *the abandonment, the lack of love, the violence.*
> *On this most barren of trails,*
> *grace falls like rain, a deep benediction.*
> *Even here, forgiveness can blossom*
> *inexplicably,*
> *like a delicate desert rose. Amen.*

FOR REFLECTION

Can you think of someone whom you have forgiven numerous times? How did it feel to keep giving someone second, tenth, or twentieth chances? What was your motivation to keep forgiving? Have you ever seen forgiveness being misused? When does forgiveness hurt a situation instead of helping?

SUNDAY

Searching for Sorries

But Esau ran to meet him and embraced him and fell on his neck and kissed him, and they wept. —Genesis 33:4

READ: Genesis 33:1–11

Have you ever gone looking for sorries in the Bible? The Bible is not about perfect people who do only good things; it contains so many stories of brokenness. In fact, family breakdown stories are a dime a dozen, especially in the Hebrew Bible.

I went searching for the places where people confess their sin to each other. I did not find:

Cain saying, "Mom and Dad, I'm sorry; I killed your son, my brother Abel."

Lot saying, "Uncle Abram, I took advantage of you, taking the better part of land for myself. I'm sorry."

Sarah saying, "Hagar, I mistreated you; I exploited and abused you. It was my fault."

Rebekah saying, "Esau, my son, I conspired against you. I'm sorry; I failed you as a mother."

Laban saying, "Isaac, I deceived you, and it was the wrong thing to do. I'm sorry."

Amnon saying to Tamar, "Tamar, my sister, I violated you, and it was wrong. I'm sorry."

Absalom saying to David, "Dad, I've messed up and hurt you. I'm sorry; I regret it deeply."

Why are there so few sorries? When I think about all the conflicts I know of in my own extended family, most of my family members never said or received sorries either. Maybe the biblical ratio of problems to sorries isn't that out of whack.

In families that are functioning well, saying "I'm sorry" is a regular part of the vocabulary of love. We see we messed up, we want to make things right, and a good apology (followed by actions that show our sincerity) is the foundation of loving one another.

In healthy relationships, we also have patience with those we love. In my family, we talk about how many problems could be solved with a snack and a nap, so we don't take offense when someone snaps at us due to being hungry or overtired. We give some allowances for a bad day, a bad week, a bad month, and even a bad year. Sometimes we know that it will take some time for an apology to happen. The person in the wrong needs to cool down, or to gain perspective on the situation.

But some families find it very hard to say "sorry" to one another. I didn't grow up in a family where people often apologized. There was love in our family, but apologies seemed to get stuck in our parents' mouths and were never spoken, so it's not something we saw modeled at home. Working through emotion-filled conflicts is really hard for a lot of families.

When someone we love hurts us, it cuts deeply, perhaps more deeply than a stranger could ever hurt us. When we are betrayed by a family member, we can be so wounded that anger wells up like a broken water main.

Today's scripture is one of the few stories in the Bible that shows a family breakdown being mended with a sorry. Jacob acted despicably toward his twin brother, Esau. He stole his father Isaac's blessing by impersonating Esau and deceiving his father on his deathbed. Esau was so angry, he wanted to murder Jacob in response (Genesis 27:41).

However, even knowing he is in great danger, we never hear Jacob saying, "Esau, my brother, it was so wrong of me to take your inheritance. It was underhanded and mean, and I lied to our father for my own gain. I hurt you terribly, and I wish I could undo what I did." Jacob doesn't have words to offer Esau, but he has actions. He sends waves of gifts to his brother's approaching party (Genesis 32:3–21), and then he uses body language to communicate his apology: he bows seven times before Esau to show his humility. He describes himself to Esau as "your servant" (33:3–5).

We witness an amazing reunion of the estranged brothers in today's scripture passage. Jacob, the liar and cheater, had run for his life years earlier (see Genesis 27:42–28:5). What changed so that he and Esau can hug it out instead of being at odds? Did Esau forgive because of the gifts, the bowing down, the servant language?

I think those things helped, but they don't explain the situation fully. I think something changed in Esau's heart long before this meeting. An essential component is that Esau is not suffering. Jacob may have cheated him out of what he deserved from his father as the firstborn son, but Esau has prospered anyway. He is a leader, he has a family, and things have fallen out for him in pleasant places. From this vantage point of well-being, forgiveness may come more easily.

Imagine if Jacob's lies and thievery had left Esau so destitute that he couldn't afford to marry. Imagine if he was the laughingstock of his community because he was duped. If Esau was still living in misery years later, alone and disadvantaged, I don't think Jacob's arrival, preceded by a display of the expensive gifts he could afford and how many wives and children he had, would have helped the situation.

Instead I think Esau's forgiveness of Jacob has come with time. Things turned out prosperously for both of them, and so decades later the good memories surface and they can hug and reminisce.

Time and circumstances don't always yield the fruit of reconciliation. For example, as described in earlier sessions, we don't see a reunion like this between Tamar and her family. Absalom and Amnon are dead. King David could have reunited with his daughter and showed that he cares about her. But the Bible is silent; we don't know whether David ever said anything to his daughter about her assault or apologized for his failure to do anything about it.

As Tamar's story reminds us, people don't always find a way toward saying they are sorry. God calls us, when it is in our power, to try to apologize. Not everyone will respond to that call, and not all of our stories will have happy resolutions in this world. But God also walks with us on thorny paths of unresolved pain. We do not search for sorries alone.

> **PRAY:** *God, it can be so hard to find the right words.*
> *Apologies seem to be stuck inside us;*
> *we don't know how to give birth to them.*
> *We keep thinking that maybe we aren't at fault,*
> *or we want someone else to apologize first.*
> *But grace is growing in us;*
> *let it be born again with a well-placed*
> *and heartfelt sorry. Amen.*

FOR REFLECTION

What are some examples of apologies you have received from people? Are there people you want an apology from who have never offered one? If you have forgiven someone without receiving an apology from them, consider the circumstances. What or who enabled you to forgive?

MONDAY

Taking Separate Paths

But Jacob journeyed to Succoth and built himself a house and made booths for his cattle; therefore the place is called Succoth.
—Genesis 33:17

READ: Genesis 33:12–20

Jacob and Esau have had the reunion of reunions. Brothers who took very different paths are finally together again. How incredible it must have been for them to hold each other after years of distance! Esau then wants to spend more time together, but Jacob is not so sure about that prospect. Jacob dawdles with his family and says he will meet up with Esau later. But time goes by and he doesn't catch up to Esau. Instead he buys a property in a place far from his brother.

Having a moment of closeness does not mean that Jacob and Esau are one big happy family again. Maybe the two boys never got along growing up; perhaps they were like oil and water. Not all family members like each other. Maybe the reunion felt good but reminded Jacob that he doesn't much like Esau's company.

Or maybe Jacob doesn't completely trust Esau. Jacob betrayed Esau in a serious way. Esau seems to forgive him, but can Jacob trust the forgiveness to hold? Jacob may wonder if aggression or bitterness is hiding under the surface.

Where does God fit into this story of Jacob and Esau's reunion? The narrator of this biblical family saga doesn't share any words of judgment or affirmation. The text doesn't say what the brothers were thinking or feeling or even what their motivations might have been in that moment. We just hear about their actions and draw our conclusions from them.

In this story, forgiveness does not mean reconciliation. There is a moment of meeting, and then the brothers depart to live their separate lives. Maybe there is just too much water over the bridge—the flood of their shared history means no one is sure whether the fragile bridge of forgiveness will hold. No one will risk crossing this river again.

When we think about coming together with friends or family after a big rift, we are in a wondering time. We wonder if apologies can happen. We wonder if reconciliation is possible. We wonder if God can provide new beginnings after the departure of someone from our life. We wonder where God is in our painful situation, and whether there can be some form of resurrection or renewal.

I have experienced broken relationships with several dear friends, for very different reasons. These rifts have been a source of great grief in my life. I have spent so many sleepless nights wondering what went wrong, or how I might repair the breach. I wonder, Has the bridge been washed away, or is it possible for the flood to recede and for connection to be reestablished? Even though decades have passed, I continue to pray and hope.

And I have had relationships where I was the one who did not want to reconcile. I had an ex-brother-in-law who died before I had reached a place where I could forgive him for how he treated my sister. So I have found myself on different ends of the estrangement spectrum, calling on God for help. I think these experiences have taught me to tread lightly as I bear witness to other people's journeys.

In my extended family, two siblings who had been extremely close endured a decade-long estrangement. When one of the siblings experienced a decline in health, the breach was repaired. We thanked God that these siblings had found peace with each other.

However, in a friend's family, such a repair didn't happen. An adult son disrespected his mother for many years and even stole a substantial amount of money from her, so she chose to break off ties with him. When the mother became terminally ill, the other siblings convinced the wayward son to come to his mother's bedside because they hoped he would make peace with her. He sat by her bed for half an hour without saying anything or reaching out to her. Then he walked away and did not return. She died a few days later.

Stories like this break our hearts. We want to hear about a tearful reconciliation and peace descending like a dove. But there are many jagged endings in this life where we can only turn to God with the shards of relationships in our hands.

Church communities are called to walk with people who find themselves in vastly different contexts. In my experience, a challenging context for the congregation can be a marital breakdown. Perhaps these breakdowns are difficult in part because we may have celebrated that couple's love in a public ceremony. We witnessed their vows and gave them God's blessing. Family ties and friendship groups in the church that supported the marriage can be affected by marital breakdown.

When a marriage ends, friends and family in the church can feel torn—should they arrange separate gatherings with each person now? Often, certain friends are drawn toward one partner, which can leave the other feeling left out and neglected. There can be tension if the former couple doesn't want to see each other, yet both want to attend the same church. I know some pastors have negotiated an every-other-Sunday policy, where divorced couples take turns coming to the same church. Even so, weddings and churchwide special occasions can be complicated.

We need God's wisdom in churches as we learn to walk with hurting people. When people cannot journey together any longer, we can support them as they go separate ways. Others need encouragement as they try to work toward reconciliation. We know that Jesus is with us in both types of situations, offering grace and love even when our grace and love falters.

> **PRAY**: *Jesus, you are an impossibility specialist.*
> *When friendships and families fracture,*
> *navigate the rapids of estrangement with us.*
> *Where possible, bring us to the healing waters of reconciliation*
> *or ready us for new beginnings.*
> *As churches, give us divine wisdom*
> *to care for all our hurting members,*
> *offering unconditional love and prayers*
> *wherever they find themselves. Amen.*

FOR REFLECTION

Why do you think Jacob and Esau took separate paths after their reunion? If you've witnessed the dissolution of a marriage or an estranged relationship in your church community, how did the larger community respond? Have you seen a church effectively support a separating couple to help them heal and move on separately?

TUESDAY

Hoping for Forgiveness

Every generous act of giving, with every perfect gift, is from above, coming down from the Father of lights. —James 1:17

READ: James 1:17–25

Sin breaks relationships. When we harm someone, we can repent and seek forgiveness from God, but we must also do the work of apologizing and being accountable to the person or people we hurt.

We can hope that forgiveness will eventually be extended to us, but we cannot demand it.

The image of the mirror in today's scripture is very powerful. If we look at ourselves in the mirror and see a person whom God has forgiven, then that image should influence our actions. A person forgiven by God should act in ways that make interpersonal forgiveness more likely. If we fail to change our behavior moving forward, we have forgotten the image in the mirror.

I attended a large church conference where a man told a terrible story. He had been a soldier in a Latin American country. As part of his duties, he had tortured many people in a military prison. Years passed, and he emigrated to Canada and became a Christian. Now he was haunted by the faces of the people he had harmed. He was feeling tortured by the torture he had inflicted. In tears, he appealed to us, "Can you forgive me for what I did?"

Immediately, a man in the crowd stood up and said, "Brother, we forgive you for what you did."

I left the meeting shaken and upset. I did feel compassion for the person who had tortured others. But he had not hurt me. I could not forgive him for the harm he had done. He needed to apologize to the people he hurt. He was addressing a group of predominantly white North Americans, and I doubt many of us had ever experienced incarceration and torture. We knew almost nothing of that type of crime or what it meant to the victims.

I can understand why that man stood up to try to offer forgiveness. It's painful to see someone in anguish, and he wanted to free that man by forgiving him. The alternative was to sit with the tension of unresolved pain and heartache. But that is the reality this soldier had created by torturing people. Even though we may have longed to, we could not rescue him from the consequences of his own behavior. We could have said, "Have you sought the forgiveness of God, which is available to all who repent? We care for you, we hear your pain, and we want to support you as you seek forgiveness from the people you harmed."

Churches must be careful about offering forgiveness out of turn. Consider the story of a pastor who had treated the church's music director unprofessionally. She belittled the music director in front of others, and when they were alone, she regularly yelled at him. During a difficult meeting, the pastor picked up a cup of pencils from the desk and threw it at the music director. All this led to the music director making a formal complaint to the church. An investigation found that the pastor had committed misconduct. Her credentials were suspended and she went for counseling. Two months later, the church council issued a statement publicly forgiving the pastor and welcoming her back.

But the pastor had never apologized to the music director! The pastor had minimized and denied some of the charges in the misconduct investigation, blaming the music director all while outwardly seeking forgiveness from the church. She was eager to resume her leadership role. Unfortunately, the church council had never consulted the music director to seek his opinion about the pastor's return.

We can't forgive people if we are not the ones harmed. We can support the person who wants forgiveness, and can encourage them to be patient and work on restitution. Viewing human forgiveness as a gift that will come in God's good time can help. Forgiveness can grow in a person like an unborn baby. Demanding that someone produce forgiveness is like asking a pregnant woman to give birth right now, even though she has just found out she is pregnant. Just because we want to see the baby doesn't mean it's time for the baby to be born. When will it be born? Only God knows. We can provide nourishing food and safety to the hurting person, but we cannot give birth to that baby for them.

What if the person we harmed is holding a grudge and has sworn never to forgive us? When we harm people, we do not control whether they will forgive us. The only thing we can do is pray for those we harmed and continue to do the work of showing we are sorry.

A person who drove under the influence of drugs causes a car crash that kills someone in the other car. The driver apologizes, and even offers to pay the medical bills for another passenger who was hurt in the accident when their bills aren't covered by insurance. Further actions can show the driver's ongoing remorse, like deciding not to touch drugs again or going into schools and talking about the dangers of impaired driving. Even then, those who have lost a family member may not forgive the driver, because their loss is too raw.

Knowing that God forgives us gives us an element of freedom and can console us, even as we hope and wait for forgiveness from others. God can help us live with the tension of unresolved hurts and loose ends. We can pray and trust that in God's good time, forgiveness from others may come into our lives like a gift.

PRAY: *Mother of us all,*
> *when we lose patience with how long forgiveness takes,*
> *when we feel we can never forgive someone,*
> *when we want to demand that someone forgive us,*
> *when we are irritated with jagged ends*
> *and frustrated by unresolved hurts,*
> *hold us tight.*

Your hope is growing in us,
> *pregnant with possibility,*
> *ripe with promise. Amen.*

FOR REFLECTION

Have you ever heard of someone apologizing to the wrong person because they wanted to avoid addressing the person they have actually hurt? Where does that leave the wronged party? Has someone demanded forgiveness from you when you weren't ready to give it? Does the metaphor of forgiveness and pregnancy resonate with you?

RESPONDING TO BROKENNESS

WEDNESDAY

Working at Repair

Against you, you alone, have I sinned and done what is evil in your sight. —Psalm 51:4

READ: Psalm 51:1–17

We once owned a house that was over a century old. I was washing the dishes one night when I heard a deep, loud bang right beneath where I stood, and the whole floor moved down beneath my feet, just slightly. This was so startling, I ran to tell my family, "Something very, very bad has just happened to our house!" We went downstairs immediately to investigate.

The house was held up by original big wooden beams in the basement, which were helped along their length by metal support posts. One of these metal posts underneath where I was standing had gradually been rusting away, and then in one dramatic moment it collapsed.

If I had not felt the bang, we might not have seen that the post behind the washing machine had crumpled. The whole house would have started sagging, and eventually we would have noticed walls cracking and other damage. But we responded immediately to the brokenness we discovered and had a new support post installed right away.

How do we respond to brokenness when we first perceive it? We can ignore it—"Bang, what bang?" We can perform a really quick survey, and leave it at that—"I don't see any problem here." Or we can put off fixing the problem—"Maybe next week I'll get to that, or when I have some holiday time. It will be fine till then." Or we can take the brokenness very seriously indeed, drop everything else, and do the hard work of repair.

At the top of Psalm 51 in my Bible, the NRSV translation says, "A psalm of David, when the prophet Nathan came to him, after he had gone in to Bathsheba."

You can read about what David did in 2 Samuel 11 and 12. He took advantage of Bathsheba, one of the wives of his soldiers. She had no one to protect her, because her husband Uriah was away at war, fighting for David. She had no choice when King David called her to join him.

Imagine her quandary. Her husband's life is in David's hands. If she resists David's sexual advances, he could easily arrange to have her husband killed. I could imagine her going along with David's expressed desires to protect her husband. Yet in the end, David specifically arranges that Uriah be killed to cover up David's crime against Bathsheba. David premeditates murder and uses the tool of his enemy's hands to orchestrate the plan. All for his own selfish gain.

The big bang in David's life, when the floor drops from under him, is when the prophet Nathan confronts him and names his sin. David is repentant, according to 2 Samuel 12, and this song in Psalm 51 is listed as David's response.

I am uncomfortable with the phrase "against you, you alone, have I sinned" (Psalm 51:4). Yes, in the larger picture of things, every wrong we commit is a sin against God's design for us. But our sins do not just affect God—they materially affect other people as well. In this case, David's sins affect Uriah, who is dead. And Bathsheba, who was sexually coerced. Both are unnamed in this song.

Samuel points out to David how the rot of his actions led to these disastrous consequences. The rust of self-centeredness has been eroding his kingship. David had been crowned king to be a pillar for the people of Israel, to protect them and support them. Instead, he did what was right in his own eyes, and things are falling apart in disastrous ways as a result.

David is confessing to God here, but he isn't doing the hard work of putting that new post in place. We see no acknowledgment of and no apologies to the people he hurt. It seems to me that a new and right spirit is definitely needed in David's life, and it isn't there yet.

What can we learn from David's situation when we hear big bangs in our own lives? We are fortunate if we have a prophet who will spell out what we have done wrong. Unfortunately, we don't usually like to listen to prophets. We tend to ignore them, mock them, or pretend they are wrong about us; that part of human nature remains the same as it was in the time of the biblical prophets.

David was wise enough to listen to the prophet Nathan, which perhaps explains something about him being referred to as a man after God's own heart. There was humility there when David admitted he made mistakes. That is an important quality. By God's grace, we will hopefully develop that humility in our own lives. We need to figure out what tasks are most important to do first when we are faced with our own sin. Who needs help, who needs apologies? Talking to the person we've harmed and seeing what they need is key: "How can I start to make things right with you? What do you need?"

Sometimes a prophet in our life is a pastor who helps us think about the guilt we are feeling. A counselor or therapist can help us deconstruct events in our lives. Where did we go wrong? Who was affected by our actions and words? What choices would we make differently now?

There is hope for us if we name the brokenness and get to work. If we don't respond to a crumpled post? Our lives will show more and more cracks. I know someone who literally had the back corner of their house collapse because of an unsound foundation. They had to move out while the structure was made safe. The repairs cost them tens of thousands of dollars. Far better to address brokenness at the beginning stages before partial disintegration causes an even larger structural collapse.

> **PRAY:** *God, we are not all like the wise man*
> *who built his house on the rock;*
> *we are too often like the foolish man who built on sand.*
> *We live with crumbling foundations.*
> *When things fall apart, be our architect.*
> *You come with a brand-new site plan,*
> *custom designed just for us.*
> *Your plan has a very detailed building code:*
> *our cornerstone is Jesus. Amen.*

FOR REFLECTION

Think about a time when someone pointed out something you were doing wrong. Was that person right? How did you react to that prophet at the time? How long did it take for you to respond to the reality of your situation?

Disrupting Systems

He has told you, O mortal, what is good, and what does the LORD require of you but to do justice and to love kindness and to walk humbly with your God? —Micah 6:8

READ: Micah 6:1–8

What happens if we are hurt by a system or an unrepentant organization that continues to hurt people? That's the question that Carrie Nation asked in 1900.[11] Heavy drinking was the norm for many men at that time, and women were often abused and left destitute, since they had no legal standing in the courts to oppose their husbands or partners. Nation saw firsthand the cost of excessive alcohol consumption. Her husband died of alcoholism early on in their marriage, widowing her and leaving their young daughter without a father.

Nation was a religious woman, and for years she tried to influence people to stop drinking. Then in 1900 at the age of fifty-four, she had a vision from God directing her to confront the businesses that were profiting from drunkenness. She went to Kiowa, Kansas, entered a bar, and started smashing bottles. This began a career of dramatic protests against businesses that were profiting off of alcoholism. She would go into bars and announce, "Men, I have come to save you from a drunkard's fate," and using a hatchet, she would smash the bottles behind the bar. Nation saw herself as a prophet of God.

Her actions started a movement, with many joining her in protests against the alcohol industry. Nation called bars "murder mills" and bartenders "destroyers of men's souls." She was arrested over thirty times, and was often beaten and attacked. But she was a sympathetic figure to many since she publicly named the anger that women felt because they were absolutely fed up from suffering at the hands of drunken men. Nation was honest and blunt and not at all afraid of making a scene. She was influential in having laws about serving alcohol changed.

In our day, we too see systems that profit off of human suffering. I think of the epidemic of drug overdoses: opioid addiction is a scourge in North America that has led to protracted heartache for so many families. The figures are astronomical: in the last two decades, over six hundred thousand people have died in the United States and Canada from opioid overdoses. A large portion of those deaths came from the misuse of prescription drugs.[12]

We often blame individuals for drug addiction, but many people are prescribed addictive drugs by their doctors without careful monitoring or follow-up. Drug companies lobby and influence doctors to prescribe addictive drugs freely: doctors who prescribe the most opioids have often received large sums of money from drug companies for speaking, consulting, and service fees.[13] Do we continue to blame individuals and their moral failings for their addictions, or do we look at systems that remove barriers to addiction and profit enormously from it? Drug corporations have made billions of dollars selling these drugs, and they disregard the human costs of what they do because of the staggering profitability. In recent decades, people have started to challenge these corporations in court, to make them pay for the harm they caused.

Theologian Beverly Wildung Harrison talked about "the power of anger in the work of love."[14] She maintained that anger is appropriate and helpful in the work against injustice. While anger can be misused, it can also be a powerful force for good.

The prophet Micah asks, "What does the Lord require of you?" If we know what is right but we do nothing, we sin. We are neglecting to do justice for and with people who continue to be harmed. The challenge we face when responding to brokenness is to work for justice with passion (fuelled by the anger at injustice) while never forgetting to be kind and humble.

A member of my congregation, Hedy Sawadsky, has been a longtime activist for peace who is deeply motivated by her faith in Jesus Christ. Hedy is now in her nineties. I interviewed her not long ago about the peace work she did in the 1970s and '80s, when she devoted years of her life to witnessing together with others against the violence of nuclear weapons and militarism in the United States. "We were trying to be faithful in our time," Hedy told me. They were inspired by the Hebrew midwives (Exodus 1:15–20), the Hebrew prophets, and the disciples in the New Testament. "We were following God's Spirit, our hearts, our Scripture." She was part of a larger group of Mennonites, Quakers, and Catholic Workers who held vigil for years at nuclear facilities in Colorado and Texas, drawing attention to the sinfulness of building nuclear weapons. At the same time, the peace communities served the needy in their midst in venues like soup kitchens and hospitality houses.

Many actions of her group were undergirded by prayer and partial fasting. She and her fellow team members were careful to be kind to everyone, engaging with people who worked in the plants, encouraging them to choose more life-giving careers. Hedy valued deeply the support of her own faith community and others for these actions. When I visit Hedy now, we talk about the people for whom she continues to pray, including our local congregation and political leaders.

I am inspired by the faithfulness of people like Hedy who challenge larger systems. What can a few people do in the face of corporations and political systems? I think of the lone protester in Tiananmen Square who stood in front of a line of tanks in 1989 during protests against the Chinese government. Greta Thunberg was fifteen when she started protesting every Friday outside the Swedish Parliament in 2018 with a sign, "School Strike for Climate." She was demanding politicians take stronger actions on climate change. Prophets use creative and provocative methods to make their points. And they usually get in trouble for speaking truth. Yet unjust systems will continue to steamroll over people unless someone challenges them.

God responds to the world's brokenness by calling ordinary, everyday people to stand up to evil systems. As we disrupt corrupt systems, our challenge is to keep this work grounded in prayer and spiritual wisdom.

> **PRAY:** *Thank you, God, that you plant*
> *the seeds of disruption*
> *in every tyrant's garden,*
> *and wrenches in the works*
> *of every exploitive corporation.*
> *You do that by calling people like us*
> *to stand up for Jesus in the face of injustice,*
> *and to do it in the power of your love. Amen.*

FOR REFLECTION

Think of a system that causes a lot of harm in your country or in the world. Do you know any people of faith who are trying to disrupt this system? How might your church community use its voice to join the movement for justice?

FRIDAY

Surviving Betrayal

Even my close friend in whom I trusted, who ate of my bread, has lifted the heel against me. —Psalm 41:9

READ: Psalm 41:4–13

On the last night that Jesus ate with his disciples before he died, Jesus quoted from Psalm 41 to describe the betrayal he would face (see John 13:18).

David, named as the author of Psalm 41, knew what it was like to be betrayed by someone close to him. As 2 Samuel 15–17 recounts, one of the people who betrayed him was Ahithophel, who had been a trusted counselor. Ahithophel switched his allegiance from David when Absalom staged a coup to become king. Ahithophel asked to kill David himself, with twelve thousand warriors as backup. Absalom decided not to follow Ahithophel's advice, so David survived.

What a huge shock for David that his counselor would betray him and switch sides, but how much more shocking to hear that Ahithophel wanted to track David down and murder him himself! Psalm 41 is a prayer to God about this treachery.

Death threats against us made by someone we love are sadly not unknown in today's world. Worldwide, women are more likely to be murdered by their intimate partner than by a stranger.[15] Children are more likely to be harmed by people inside their families than people outside their families. To fear for your life from a family member is a betrayal of the highest order. In fact, harm from those we love may feel worse than harm from a stranger, because it is a betrayal of trust.

My grade five teacher, Werner Fast, grew up in Ukraine during World War II.[16] When Werner was seven years old, his father, Johann, was taken away by the police and wasn't heard from again. Werner's family had to flee in the meantime, and after a five-year refugee trek they ended up in Canada. All along the way they continued to pray for the safe return of Johann to their family. His picture hung on the wall of their new living room.

One day Werner came home from school, and the picture was missing from the wall. His tearful mother explained to him that their father was not joining them in Canada. She had received news that her husband was still in the Soviet Union and was remarried and had a new family.

Werner now had an address for his father, and he wrote a letter filled with anger and disappointment. His mother encouraged him to rewrite it with a less judgmental, more forgiving attitude, to mirror the attitude she was trying to have. Werner did as his mother advised, and over the coming years and decades, Werner kept up a correspondence with his father.

When the Iron Curtain between the Soviet Union and the West finally began to lift, Werner fulfilled the longing he felt to see his father. Forty-six years after Johann was taken away that night by the police, Werner was able to meet his father again, along with his father's new family in a tearful reunion.

On the last day of Werner's visit, Johann and his wife poured out a confession about how guilty they felt through their whole marriage. His father explained what had happened. When Johann heard that his family had emigrated to Canada, he gave up hope of ever seeing them again in this world. The Soviet border was impenetrable. He was so lonely, and he fell in love with someone and decided to make a new start. Werner confessed how angry he had been at his father, and that he didn't truly comprehend the impossible circumstances he faced. They all prayed together, asking God to take away any residue of resentment. They forgave each other for the hurt they caused.

I spoke with Werner about this story, and he told me that his mother had been hurt in many ways by many people and groups. She had suffered so much at the hands of Josef Stalin and the police, who took her husband away in the first place. Terrible things had happened on their refugee trek through a war-torn country, and they faced unkindness in Canada from people who were prejudiced against newcomers. "But," Werner told me, "the greatest pain in her life, the greatest challenge for her to forgive, was that my father remarried."

Have you ever felt betrayed by someone you loved? Perhaps a parent or a spouse let you down, or a sibling or your child betrayed you in some way. Or maybe a good friend did something that hurt you terribly. The wound from a loved one, Shakespeare wrote, is the "unkindest cut of all."[17]

Some of us lug the smarting flesh wounds of slights and snubs that don't seem to heal, and others carry weightier betrayals. I can think of one hurt in particular that still seems fresh after all these years. Bearing a memory like that is a long, quiet, intense path where we concentrate on putting our feet down very carefully one in front of the other. Yet Jesus walks with us.

Werner's mother never saw his father again, but she tried to live without resentment toward him, and she tried to forgive him. She was alive when Werner went to Russia to see Johann, and she sent along money for her former husband, asking that he buy a new suit with it. Werner gave the money to his dad, who thought he didn't need a new suit. But his family said they would use the money to buy him some new clothes.

A year later, Johann passed away. Werner called his half-brothers on the telephone to express condolences. He asked them if his father had ever used the clothes. They said he had never put them on, but the family had decided that he would be buried in his new suit.

PRAY: *God, our sorrows are weighty,*
and we can carry them for a lifetime.
The shock of betrayal retains its freshness
even as our bodies age and change.
You match our steps, stride for stride,
your right hand holds us up.
We trust that you can console the years,
in ways that we cannot always understand
or even imagine. Amen.

FOR REFLECTION

Are you bearing a deep wound that makes it hard to forgive someone? Do you anticipate carrying this burden for the rest of your life? How is God calling you to make small steps toward forgiveness?

SATURDAY

Guarding against Harm

As Jesus was walking along, he saw a man called Matthew sitting at the tax-collection station, and he said to him, "Follow me." And he got up and followed him. —Matthew 9:9

READ: Matthew 9:9–13

The job of a tax collector was to count money and keep accounts. All day every day, Matthew counted coins, keeping track of money coming in and money going out. The Romans levied sales taxes, property taxes, import and export taxes, and tolls on roads. Capernaum, where this story takes place, was on a Roman trade route between the great cities of Damascus and Caesarea, so Matthew had a lot of counting to do.

Romans recruited local Jewish men like Matthew to collect taxes, whose wages came from extra charges on top of the taxes. Tax collectors had the might of Rome behind them to punish those who didn't pay. Tax collectors were hated because they were seen as collaborators with Rome. Poor families were left poorer, and meager tables were emptier because of this oppression. Tax collectors ignored their role in causing that pain, probably thinking, "I'm only doing my job!"

People complained that Jesus was eating with "tax collectors and sinners" (Matthew 9:11). Jesus calls Matthew directly from his tax-collection booth. Jesus is willing to forgive Matthew's sin of oppressing the people by cooperating with Rome, and he welcomes him into the band of disciples.

Jesus and his disciples did not work for wages during his ministry, as far as we know, and lodging and food had to be bought. Jesus' ministry was financially supported by Mary Magdalene and other women (Luke 8:1–3); we know there must have been substantial donations, because then and now, it costs money to live.

Matthew was obviously an expert money handler, so wouldn't it have made sense to put him in charge of the cash that Jesus and the disciples carried with them? Yet Jesus did not choose Matthew. It was Judas who controlled the purse for the group (John 12:6). If Jesus had forgiven Matthew's sins, why didn't he put him in charge of the money?

I wonder whether Jesus did not want to put Matthew into temptation's way. Matthew had been drawn into the world of extortion; greed was likely a major problem for him. Asking Matthew to hold a bag of donations might be too risky. Old habits die hard, and he might be tempted to skim the donations, just as he skimmed money off the taxes.

I also wonder whether it was for the donors' sakes that Jesus did not put Matthew in charge of the money. For years, people had resentfully given their hard-earned money to Matthew in his tax booth, and he had taken advantage of them. I suspect people would not feel comfortable handing their donations for Jesus' ministry into Matthew's hands.

Imagine that one of your church members, an accountant, committed financial crimes and stole from her business clients. When she is tried, sentenced, and released from prison, this congregant is completely repentant, and people do forgive her. But does forgiving her mean you would elect her as church treasurer? We may truly believe people are repentant, yet we would be wise not to put them in temptation's way. And if we want people to donate to the church, we need our financial people to be above reproach.

In our communities, we want to care for everyone. Caring can mean that we consider people's weaknesses and avoid dangling temptation in front of them. For example, you wouldn't ask a friend who is a recovering alcoholic to pour the wine at your dinner party. You want to keep them out of harm's way, so you probably wouldn't even serve alcohol at the party if you knew your friend would be coming.

One of the areas I've studied extensively is pastoral sexual misconduct. There is often a common pattern to how churches respond. When a complaint about sexual misconduct by a pastor is received, the church is often shocked. "How could our loving and wise pastor abuse someone?" Many times, churches blame the victim or discount their story. But if evidence is found in the investigation that something terrible did happen, churches might quietly ask for the resignation of the pastor. They offer the pastor forgiveness, but also require the pastor to leave. Sometimes churches even give the pastor a good reference to help them get another job.

People may be well-intentioned and want to give the pastor another chance. "We don't want to ruin the pastor's life!" they may say. However, if the pastor goes to another church and suddenly there are five more victims, do the good intentions outweigh the disastrous effect? What is more important, giving the pastor another chance, or protecting vulnerable people and keeping them out of harm's way? Chillingly, the congregation does not trust the pastor enough to continue employing them, but they give a good reference, thus endangering another community. This forgive-and-forget mentality is dangerous.

If you were physically abused by a parent during childhood, as an adult, you may have come to some sort of resolution with that parent in your adulthood. They may have admitted their sin, apologized, and you may even have forgiven them. But that kind of relational repair does not mean that you would let them babysit your own children. Doing so could put your kids in potential danger. Forgiving does not mean forgetting. Establishing a boundary like this can cause tension. Your parents may say, "If you have truly forgiven us, you would let us babysit. We are different people now!" It is your responsibility to prioritize your children's safety over proving something to your parents or letting them have the opportunity to prove something to you.

Forgiveness does not mean we are naïve or insensitive to potential danger. It means we can be as "wise as serpents and innocent as doves" (Matthew 10:16). We balance forgiveness with caution—we guard against further harm. We create a culture of accountability that makes our communities safer.

PRAY: *Our Father,*
    lead us not into temptation,
    and be with us as we make decisions
    about not leading others into temptation.
  Help us to prioritize protecting the vulnerable
    rather than maximizing the freedom of those
    who have abused their power. Amen.

FOR REFLECTION

Can you think of someone who caused harm, made apologies, and desires to return to a former position or relationship? How can boundaries be put in place to help protect that person from the temptation to sin again? How can boundaries be established to protect others from future harm?

SUNDAY

Confronting with Wisdom

If another member of the church sins against you, go and point out the fault when the two of you are alone. —Matthew 18:15 (NRSV)

READ: Matthew 18:15–22

After church one Sunday, Lana says to Ray, "You are such a hero working with those seniors." The words themselves were appreciative, but Ray hears sarcasm in the tone of her voice, and he complains about it to a few people the next week. Word gets back to Lana. She calls him and says, "You thought I was being sarcastic, and so your feelings were hurt. I truly do admire you for your work with seniors—you are making a real difference. I wasn't being sarcastic, and I'm sorry that my words came across that way."

This conflict and gossip could have been avoided if Ray had gone to Lana himself right off the bat. He could have said, "Lana, I want to check in with you about something. When you said *x*, I am just wondering what you meant. I left the conversation feeling hurt." If we fail to confront the person who did the harm, we are sidestepping the possibility of repentance. We all make mistakes, and having them pointed out can often clear things up.

However, it is not always safe to confront a person who causes offense. When one person has power over another, confronting that person could be harmful for the person who was hurt. But when an

offense is caused by a person with whom one feels on equal foot-
ing, not confronting the person who caused harm and drawing in
other people can expand the issue, making it bigger than it already
was. The problem becomes more complicated to solve, because now
instead of one angry person, there are four angry people.

Matthew 18 counsels that if we are unsuccessful at dealing with
something privately, we can "take one or two others along" with us
(v. 16). As opposed to, in modern times, posting it on social media so
our three hundred friends can all be mad at this person too!

These verses provide helpful advice for responding to certain
kinds of problems between church members. But as noted above, this
process is not appropriate for every situation, especially ones that
involve certain harms. Consider this scenario: Adolfo and Janna are
youth sponsors on a weekend youth retreat. After the first overnight,
Janna is pulled aside by a tearful fifteen-year-old girl, Regina. She
explains that during the night a fifteen-year-old boy, Ben, crawled
into her sleeping bag, and did things she didn't want him to do.

Janna goes to talk privately to Adolfo. His idea is that Regina
should go alone to talk to Ben. "Last night she could have yelled and
we would have heard her, but she didn't," says Adolfo. "Maybe this
morning she is feeling bad about what they did. They should talk
it out."

Janna feels very differently. She knows that Regina is too upset
to talk to Ben. Janna thinks they need to call the parents of both
kids right away, and then she adds, "Should we call Child Protective
Services? Something bad has happened here, and we need to call in
people who have expertise about this."

Adolfo is adamant. "We can't blow this out of proportion. We
don't want Ben to have this hanging over his future when it was just
a fifteen-minute mistake. We can find a solution without making this
a bigger deal."

This scenario is not a time for following the counsel of Matthew 18. As people working with youth, sponsors Janna and Adolfo have a duty to report any sexual harm done to minors. It's not their place to judge what happened or intervene and try to work things out. Unwanted sexual contact is sexual assault, and a victim should never be expected to go and talk to the person who harmed them (alone or otherwise).

There are many other situations in the church where these verses from Matthew 18 should not be used to direct a person's next steps in conflict resolution. Whenever there is a power imbalance, it is not appropriate to expect the person with less power to confront the person with more power. Age, gender, size, sexual orientation, race, economic status, role or position, mental health challenges, and many other factors all play into why it can be impossible for two people to meet as equals and talk it out.

I have heard of too many situations where churches applied these verses from Matthew 18 in a legalistic way and the process caused even more harm than the original problem. If someone has been bullied, it is harmful for the hurt person go alone and face the bully. The church should help vulnerable people, not put them in situations where they are likely to be hurt again. Sometimes it may be appropriate for "one or two others" to join the hurt person in confronting the person who caused harm. Sometimes that is unwise. Most church members do not have conflict mediation skills and do not know how to intervene when a conversation turns toxic and hurtful.

There are situations where people can and should talk to each other to resolve conflicts. Clarifying what happened and stating one's feelings can create the opportunity for apologies and repentance. I can find this difficult, because I would far rather avoid conflict. I have been guilty of talking about people who hurt my feelings instead of addressing them directly.

But especially when there are power imbalances, we have to think carefully, to see whether one party is being disadvantaged or pressured. We need to work for peace between people, but we need to do so wisely.

PRAY: *God grant us the peace to ask for help*
when we cannot confront alone,
courage to confront those we can,
and the wisdom to know the difference.
Help us protect the most vulnerable
and hold people to account for harm they've done.
Holy Wisdom, help us do the work of justice
in a spirit of kindness and love. Amen.

FOR REFLECTION

Can you think of a specific situation where it was not safe for an individual to confront someone who caused them harm? If there was a power imbalance, how might the harm be addressed safely? Have you seen a community helping in such situations? How might a fear of conflict contribute to our unwillingness to confront?

MONDAY

Extending Mercy

So my heavenly Father will also do to every one of you, if you do not forgive your brother or sister from your heart. —Matthew 18:35

READ: Matthew 18:23–35

Much of the time, we live in a tit-for-tat world. Some families can keep meticulous scorecards. You yelled at me last month, and I don't forget that. So if I hurt you this week by not including you in a social event, then in my mind we are even. That is, until the next slight rolls around.

Today's parable from Matthew 18 upends the tit-for-tat world. A servant owes the king ten thousand talents, which is an astronomical sum of money, years of wages for a common laborer. With a simple appeal for mercy, this servant's debt is forgiven. The scorecard is wiped clean. What an amazing gift of generosity on the part of the king!

The servant who had the enormous sum of money erased turns around and, seeing someone who owes him money, seizes him by the throat, saying, "Pay what you owe!" Word gets back to the king, who comes and challenges the unforgiving servant in a dramatic way, reminding him about all that was forgiven.

The king had introduced mercy into the tit-for-tat world. The servant liked that arrangement as long as he was the one benefiting. When mercy would benefit someone else, he was back to business as usual.

A death in the family can often prompt family members to tally and compare scorecards, even if only subconsciously. There can be deep hurt if one child was favored over another, if there was unfinished business, or if a will seems unfair. Think of the ill will generated when the biblical character Isaac was dying. Jacob tried to even up a scorecard that felt tipped in his brother's favor. Disaster resulted.

On one side of my family, a grandfather remarried very near the end of his life, and he married a woman who was close in age to his own children. When he died, he had no will, so his estate automatically went to his new wife and not to the eight children who had hoped to inherit their father's money. This was unfortunate from the children's point of view.

To add insult to what they perceived as injury, one of the daughters approached the wife and said, "I wonder whether I might have as a keepsake the pink sugar bowl that sat on the kitchen table. That was our mother's sugar bowl, and it has a lot of sentimental value for me." The wife was unwilling to share it. "I really like that sugar bowl myself," she said.

I heard this story numerous times from different people. For members of that side of the family, the new wife's behavior went beyond the pale; the one who had inherited everything was unwilling to share even a tiny shred of the estate.

On another side of my family there was a longstanding grievance between a father and his son. There was no love lost, and they had almost nothing to do with each other. When the father died, one might think that the score was settled finally; there could be no more hurts. However, the stepmother in this case wrote the obituary and published it in the newspaper. The obituary listed all the children the man had—except the estranged son's name was left off of the list of children. The final power move in the game was simply erasing the son's name from the scorecard as if he didn't exist.

People living in a tit-for-tat world assume that everything is quantifiable and measurable. The concept of mercy challenges such assumptions: it doesn't just want to rearrange the numbers on the chart, it wants to throw away scorecards. The final words of Jesus' parable suggest that a change of heart is needed. Instead of adding up pluses and minuses, the scorecards melt away in the light of love.

Imagine a world where when a father dies, an olive branch is extended to the estranged son, who is invited home with an obituary that reads, "He is survived by his beloved son . . .". At the time of death, we look back at someone's life. The father certainly loved his son during his lifetime, even if things were strained at the end.

Imagine a world where someone receiving a large inheritance is happy to share from their abundance. "Of course you can have the sugar bowl! Are there other mementos that are important to you?"

Mercy and grace are the marvelous gifts of Jesus. He gave so much to us and was himself a gift from a God who gives "generously and ungrudgingly" (James 1:5). When the Spirit fills our hearts with empathy toward one another, the "yours" and "mine" categories fade into the background. Instead of holding grudges, we are primed to be generous.

Where does this parable leave the people with great hurts and unresolved tragedies? Are they doomed to be condemned by God because they don't achieve forgiveness in this life? Jesus didn't demand forgiveness of people who were in pain. He didn't turn to the woman who was almost stoned to death and say, "You must forgive those men who wanted to kill you." Instead Jesus said, "Neither do I condemn you" (John 8:11). Jesus didn't tell the man being crucified next to him on a cross, "You must forgive these crucifiers." Instead he said, "Today you will be with me in paradise" (Luke 23:43).

God gives good gifts and doesn't expect impossible things from people who are terribly hurt. But God does expect that in the ordinary hurly-burly of life, we should have a loving attitude and a forgiving spirit toward those who slight us. We are invited to extend mercy to others in the same way we've received God's mercy.

> **PRAY:** *When we want to add and subtract hurts and slights,*
> *generous God, multiply grace within us.*
> *When we want to carry grudges and spite,*
> *Jesus, show us your merciful way.*
> *Transform us through your Spirit of love*
> *working in us, each and every day. Amen.*

FOR REFLECTION

Are there emotional scorecards in your life where you keep accounts of who has hurt you and how much? Can you think of ways to abandon scorekeeping and adopt a more generous attitude? Or perhaps you know someone has kept careful score of your slights. What would it mean to have those erased permanently?

Breathing Hope

I will put my spirit within you, and you shall live. —Ezekiel 37:14

READ: Ezekiel 37:1–14

In today's reading the people of Israel in exile in Babylon are separated from their land, their temple, and their autonomy. Some generations have passed, and none of the Israelites have ever even seen Jerusalem. Should they give up on going home? God helps them keep that hope alive by giving Ezekiel the vision of the dry bones.

Ezekiel's vision helps Christians today too. We interpret this story through the lens of Jesus, who as the firstborn of the dead, will raise us up on the last day.

Theologian Allen Callahan describes how important Ezekiel's vision has been and is to Black churches in the United States, particularly as a popular text featured in sermons and religious songs.[18] Enslaved in America and in exile from their home, generations of Black people longed for a rush of the Holy Spirit to bring life in the living death of their enslavement. As racist oppression continues beyond the formal abolishment of slavery, this vision still resonates.

Ezekiel's vision has been influential in so many radically different contexts, conveying the message that God can and does work miracles in our lives. Have you seen God bringing life to places where you had no hope?

In my life, my relationship with my stepmother was something I thought was a valley of dry bones. For so many decades there was a loop of pain and resentment in my head. I prayed for help. I remember the day a counselor asked me the revolutionary question, "What was it like for a forty-year-old woman to suddenly have three stepdaughters between the ages of eight and twelve?"

It may seem like a simple, straightforward question, but I had never asked it before. It helped me journey to an earlier version of my stepmother. What made her the way she was? What was her family of origin like, and how did it shape her behavior? Though I found some empathy for her through the counseling process, her ongoing difficult behavior still made it hard for me to see her more than a few times a year.

When she was seventy-six, my stepmother suffered two broken hips within six months and could not live independently. As her next of kin, I helped her move to a long-term care home. There her difficult behavior became an issue for the nursing staff and other residents. They called in a geriatric psychiatrist, who prescribed medication to help with my stepmother's depression, aggression, and paranoid thoughts.

With the right mental health medication, my stepmother was reborn. She lived six more years in the nursing home, and I never saw her happier. She was relaxed and social, where she used to be reclusive and miserable. I think about how little information on mental illness was available to my stepmother in the 1960s when I first got to know her. How might her whole life have been different if she had access to the help she needed?

My relationship with my stepmother was transformed, and we could finally enjoy each other's company. But the past remained something we could not talk about. My stepmother only remembered good things; my memories were more troubled. I would never get an apology from her, so mostly what I did was concentrate on helping my stepmother in the present, where we could be kind to each other, and let the past go. Because God breathed on that relationship of dry bones, we could say "I love you" to each other and mean it. It took a long time for that miracle to happen, but it did happen. It has been the most surprising thing in my life.

Welcome Inn Church was a small congregation in the east end of Hamilton, Ontario. The pastor, Harry Nigh, had contact with a man named Charlie Taylor who lived with intellectual disabilities. He was being released from prison after serving a sentence for child sexual abuse, and was thought to be at high risk of reoffending. Taylor asked whether he could join the church. Was Welcome Inn Church going to welcome him?

The church talked it over, and they decided that God was calling them to extend a hand of fellowship. Taylor had been despised and rejected most of his life, at first because of his disability, and later for his crimes. The church wanted to help him make good choices and never hurt another child. They surrounded him with a group of volunteers who helped him find housing and work, and they offered friendship and support. Child safety was a priority, and so Taylor only attended services in a limited way and with careful supervision. But he was part of the church community, interacting with adults in small groups. There was a negative backlash from the surrounding community, who didn't want Taylor in their neighborhood, but the church persevered.

Taylor died a decade later; he did not reoffend.[19] The church's method for supporting Taylor was developed into a model, and then into a program that continues to operate today. It's called Circles of Support and Accountability. The purpose is to help people coming out of prison who have sexually offended and are at high risk of reoffending, and the overall goal is that these individuals would not reoffend. This program has spread to other countries around the world, helping people who had no hope find another chance in life. Circles of Support and Accountability has prevented harm to children. Volunteers have also been transformed as they work with people on the extreme margins of society.

Somehow, God was able to breathe life into all these dry bones. God's Spirit hovers over all our deep places and breathes hope.

PRAY: *Holy Spirit, deep calls to deep.*
Our deepest sorrows and deepest pains cry out to you;
   you hear us calling.
Our deepest brokenness leaves us bewildered in the wilderness,
   you offer a map and hope.
You are with us on the long journey,
   the breath of life within us. Amen.

FOR REFLECTION

Have you ever experienced a surprising twist in your life, when God brought new life to a place you thought was dead and buried? Has a broken relationship ever been restored? Reflect on that experience, examining and appreciating the power of God to change us.

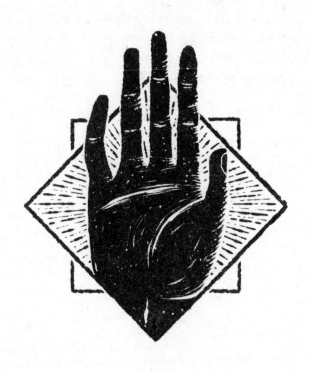

WEEK 5

BUILDING
FORGIVENESS

WEDNESDAY

Being Transformed

The wind blows where it chooses, and you hear the sound of it, but you do not know where it comes from or where it goes. So it is with everyone who is born of the Spirit. —John 3:8

READ: John 3:1–9

The Spirit is moving like the wind in the life of Nicodemus. It blows Nicodemus out of his comfortable house to a late-night conversation with Jesus. I wonder whether Nicodemus chose that time because he was worried about being seen with Jesus in the day.

The wind of the Spirit later pushes Nicodemus up to his feet to speak in a group where threatening words are winning (John 7:50–51). He may have been going out on a limb as the odd man out defending Jesus. And the Spirit leads Nicodemus to the saddest task of all: carrying Jesus' broken body to the tomb (John 19:38–39). Nicodemus performs this intimate task faithfully, but he is likely taking a risk to do it. Will he be associated with Jesus' radical ideas, or be denounced himself? Through all of these experiences, Nicodemus is slowly being transformed. Being born is not a comfortable experience for a baby, and being born again is likely uncomfortable for Nicodemus too.

The power of God to change our lives completely was an important message in the Hebrew Bible. As Samuel anoints Saul to be king of Israel, he says the Spirit of God will turn Saul "into a different person" (1 Samuel 10:6). The Hebrew word to describe this process is *hapak*. It can have many different meanings, but *hapak* often means a very big, radical change. It's the verb used by the prophet Jonah when he talks about how God is going to *hapak*, or overthrow, Nineveh (Jonah 3:4); the whole city repents. In Jeremiah 31:13, we read that God is going to *hapak* mourning into gladness. God's Spirit works in us; individuals and groups are transformed.

Ray Anderson was the founder and CEO of a huge company called Interface, one of the leading manufacturers of modular floor coverings. Anderson was very successful in business, both in terms of growing the company and making money.

One day Anderson came upon a book, *The Ecology of Commerce* by Paul Hawken. He flipped it open and randomly started reading. He read ten pages. Reading it, said Anderson, "was a like a spear to my chest." The book said that companies were plundering the earth and taking what was not theirs, spoiling the world for future generations. Anderson realized that the book was talking about him—he was one of those plunderers. Anderson was changed—in fact, he was overthrown.

From that moment on Anderson devoted himself to revolutionizing his company through sustainable business practices. He committed to ecological friendliness. His watchwords became reduce, reuse, reclaim, recycle, and redesign. He aimed as much as possible for zero scrap into landfills and zero emissions. After reading ten pages, decades of destructive patterns of behavior were overthrown and a new direction was set, not just for Anderson personally but for his company as well.

Anderson encouraged other industries to also take up this cause and freely shared his ideas about sustainability in talks to corporations and organizations. After Anderson's death in 2011, the Ray C. Anderson Foundation was established in his memory, with the mission of encouraging corporate ecological sustainability.

Anderson did not describe what he called his "mid-course correction" in religious terms in anything I've read, but the moral values of his Christian faith were undoubtedly an underlying foundation. I see God's Spirit at work in Anderson, convicting and changing him and helping him to be born again as someone who cared for the environment.[20]

Another person who experienced a wholesale change was theologian and Catholic priest Henri Nouwen. Nouwen was an influential writer and professor who taught at Yale and Harvard in the 1960s and '70s. Nouwen's classes were filled to overflowing, and his devotional books were bestsellers. He gave many lectures around the world, and people flocked to hear him.

Right in the middle of all that professional success, Nouwen was filled with doubts. He wasn't sure he was where God wanted him to be. He listened and prayed, and eventually he followed a call to become a pastor to L'Arche Daybreak Community in Toronto, Ontario. L'Arche communities are group homes where people with mental and physical challenges are welcomed as core members of a community.[21]

At L'Arche, in addition to being the community's pastor, Nouwen was responsible for the personal care of a core member. Nouwen found he was not particularly good at caregiving, and the core member he worked with let him know that. He missed the affirmation and praise he had received as a professor. He slipped into a deep depression and couldn't even leave his room for many months. But the people he had come to minister to instead ministered to him during his bout with mental illness, and he gradually recovered.

Some of the brokenness that Nouwen needed to address in his life was his love of power and prestige. God called him away from those trappings and found Nouwen a humble spot where he could serve. Nouwen later acknowledged that some of the brokenness in his life was prejudice toward people with disabilities and a patronizing feeling of superiority. Nouwen initially felt that he was making a big sacrifice to help this group that was suffering; instead, God revealed to him his own neediness.[22]

The wind of the Holy Spirit blew Nouwen to exactly the place he needed to be to learn what God wanted to teach him. He was overthrown; he was transformed.

PRAY: *Holy Spirit, you are in the soft breeze,*
the steady northerlies, the stiff gale,
and even in the tornado.
Thank you for nudging us, pushing us,
and bodily moving us
to where we are most likely to be transformed.
As we listen to the wind in the trees,
or hear it howling in the storm,
we remember our windswept moments
where we found ourselves born again
through your limitless grace. Amen.

FOR REFLECTION
Do you know anyone who was overthrown by God, with the Holy Spirit sending them in an entirely different direction? If the person you are thinking about is you, reflect on how your life might be different if God had not intervened.

THURSDAY

Supporting Accountability

They tie up heavy burdens, hard to bear, and lay them on the shoulders of others; but they themselves are unwilling to lift a finger to move them. —Matthew 23:4

READ: Matthew 23:1–12

Jesus feels the heaviness of the burdens that people are carrying. He delivers strong woeful words to the scribes and Pharisees who make rules so burdensome that few can follow them.

Historically, Christians have used the specific criticisms in Matthew 23 to characterize all Jewish people, and this negative stereotyping was part of the justification to persecute and kill Jews, including during the Holocaust. But Jesus is not calling for violence; he is calling for accountability. Jesus would love for the religious leaders to repent. Accountability never negates forgiveness; they go hand in hand. Accountability can set the stage for forgiveness.

Who is suffering in this story? It's the people, and they are suffering under the religious burdens put upon them. Jesus doesn't say to these burdened people, "You must forgive the Pharisees." Instead, he focuses on the most powerful group, asking them to change their behavior. It's their job to start building steps up the wall of sin that separates them from the common people.

Another passage of scripture that talks about heavy burdens is found in Exodus 5, where we hear how the people of Israel were enslaved in Egypt. They are being worked to the bone, and that's when the Egyptian taskmasters heap up even more work for them. Now they have to make the same number of bricks, but also collect the raw material to make them. To add to their suffering, Pharaoh looks at these people slaving in the heat and calls them lazy (Exodus 5:17)!

Burdening those who are already burdened is something churches have done too. Forgiveness has been treated as a law to be obeyed no matter what; people have been told they must forgive even when they are still being abused or hurt. Giving this message is the equivalent of throwing a concrete block instead of a life preserver toward a drowning person and saying, "Catch this and stop drowning!" It is almost impossible to forgive someone while they are hurting you. And if forgiving someone sidesteps accountability and enables them to keep hurting you, it is dangerous.

I have walked with survivors of domestic violence, and I have heard their stories of what they experienced in church communities. It's usually very upsetting for church leaders to hear that one of their own families is experiencing physical, sexual, or emotional violence. Understandably, the church leaders wish the violence was not happening. But their distress can be misplaced; they may feel that the abuse casts a bad light on the whole congregation. They want this problem to go away, so sometimes they immediately go to the abusing person and ask, "Are you sorry for what you did?" Of course, that person will say they are sorry. Then leaders will go to the person who is being hurt and say, "The person who hurt you is sorry, so just forgive and we can put this all behind us." Church leadership believes they have taken care of business, even though they have minimized the accountability and restoration process.

Unfortunately, the person who is experiencing abuse has to deal not only with the pain of abuse and the fear of being abused again, but also the spiritual burden of feeling like a sinner because they can't do what their church says they must do. "Just forgive" makes it sound easy when it is not. Like the religious leaders in today's scripture passage, the church appears unwilling to lift a finger to unburden anyone.

I think this approach also burdens the person doing harm. The wrongdoer may feel relief that leaders in the church believe their sorry words, and they are happy that the leaders convinced their abused family member to forgive and to stay. However, the wrongdoer is trapped in a cycle of abusing. The church is not helping them break that cycle—they are enabling its continuation! The church keeps delivering the spouse or family member(s) into the hands of the abusing person, who continues to sin.

Relief comes from the church that helps deliver the family out of harm's way by holding the person doing the harm accountable: "You have not loved, honored, and cherished your family. We support the decision of your family to find a place of safety. We care for you, which is why we are telling you to get help so that you can stop harming others."

Around the world, certain people groups continue to suffer under the weight of harmful and systemic burdens. On Turtle Island, renamed by some as the United States and Canada, white settlers stole the land from Indigenous peoples in the name of God and their political leaders. They did everything they could to destroy the culture and heritage of Indigenous peoples. On the Great Plains, they committed genocide not just by murdering tribes with military troops but also through starvation; settlers killed the great herds of buffalo for the express purpose of starving the people who relied on them for food.

When the topic of Indigenous land sovereignty comes up, white people are too often ready to say, "That happened so long ago. Why are you are still talking about it?" Christians have often suggested that Indigenous peoples need to forgive and move on.

Except the past has not passed. The consequences of the giant land grab from previous centuries are still being felt. Indigenous peoples were confined to small, often inferior spaces on reserves and reservations, and white families became prosperous on the land they took. Descendants of white settlers still own the land they stole. The racism that prompted the stealing of the land continues, and Indigenous people face racist comments, actions, and policies every single day. Today, careful attention to justice and seeking accountability for past crimes may help prepare the way for forgiveness down the road, but it is not something that can or should be demanded.

Forgiveness is not a quick-fix solution that can be coerced from people by threatening them spiritually or by asserting that "God requires forgiveness." Too often, we demand forgiveness of others precisely because we are unwilling to do the hard work that Jesus is doing in this scripture: naming sin clearly. The emphasis should be on repentance, repair and accountability; these make true forgiveness more likely to happen.

PRAY: *God, we long for forgiveness*
like a hungry person longs for a meal on the table.
Just as grocery shopping, cooking,
setting the table, and inviting the guests
are part of hosting a dinner,
show us how naming sin,
repentance, repair, and accountability
are steps that make forgiveness more likely. Amen.

FOR REFLECTION

Do you know anyone who has been pressured to forgive someone who was still hurting them? How did the story turn out? Why do we feel compelled to try to force people into forgiveness? Why might that feel more comfortable to us than holding wrongdoers accountable?

FRIDAY

Fostering Forgiveness

And [Joseph] kissed all his brothers and wept upon them, and after that his brothers talked with him. —Genesis 45:15

READ: Genesis 45:1–15

This is one of the most famous forgiveness stories in the Bible, even though the word *forgiveness* is not used. Perhaps you've seen a children's Bible like the one I had growing up. I remember clearly the illustration of Joseph with his hands bound, being led off to Egypt with the camel train after being sold into slavery. He looks back, his brothers are a group in the distance. I felt for Joseph and the betrayal he experienced.

In our scripture today Joseph has a reunion with his brothers and is ready to forgive them. Why now? Four important things have happened. First, Joseph's life has turned out surprisingly well. He is wealthy and has a very important job, which would not have happened if he stayed living at home. Second, his status in Egypt means that the power relationship between him and his brothers has reversed. When he was sold into slavery, Joseph was the outnumbered younger brother. Now he holds the key to his family's survival because of his connections in Egypt. Third, time has passed. Decades. Joseph has had time to think about his brothers and prepare his heart to forgive them.

The final thing that sets the stage for forgiveness is that Joseph sets an elaborate and lengthy test for his brothers to see whether they have changed (Genesis 43). He finds that they have changed;

he observes care for their father and attention to the safety of their youngest brother.

These steps help Joseph reach the top of the wall of sin that stands between him and his brothers. A flood of empathy helps him leap over the top of the wall. Joseph did not forgive his brothers when he was chained and on his way to Egypt; the wall was simply too high then.

This story reminds me of brothers I knew. Drew grew up with three older brothers who tormented him mercilessly, throwing him around, holding his arm behind his back, putting him in chokeholds, and emotionally abusing him. His childhood was filled with pain from their bullying. For a long time he cried a lot and tried to get help from his mother. She told his brothers they needed to say sorry, but she never made the violence stop.

As an adult, Drew initially tried to pretend nothing bad happened. He minimized his childhood experiences. But denial bore a heavy cost, and eventually he admitted to himself, "My brothers messed me up." He told me once, "They really abused me, and I couldn't do anything about it. And my mother didn't know how to help me."

I was struck by the fact that Drew was not angry at his mother. She was the person who was supposed to protect him from harm, but her husband had died, and she was struggling and had addiction issues. Drew could have said, "It was all my mother's fault, and I hate her." But he had empathy for the difficult situation his mother faced, and so he responded by saying, "She didn't know how to help me."

Drew could say all this from a place of safety as an adult. He may have had very different feelings as a young person living in fear. As an adult, his tender love for his mother helped him to forgive her failings. And he chose to set up boundaries and not have his brothers in his life.

In both of these brother stories, the conditions fostered forgiveness. Unfortunately, the consequences of sin are sometimes so devastating that there are no steps possible to reach the top of the wall.

When a drunk driver kills your sister and her family, there will not be a time when you say, as Joseph was able to say, "This has all worked out for good." Perhaps you know people who are living with the terrible consequences of sin. Perhaps you know those consequences firsthand.

While I have been writing this book, every day I see stories on the news of destruction in Ukraine as the war with Russia drags on. Last week a dam was bombed, and communities were flooded as a giant reservoir suddenly poured down a river valley. The flooding looked similar to other natural disasters from hurricanes I've seen on TV, with people stranded on roofs of houses waiting to be rescued. Except in this situation, as helpers came in on boats and were rescuing people, bombs started dropping from the sky. Somehow that image just broke me; how low can human beings go? I was flooded with despair. God, where is your relief?

The atrocities of war and the depravity of human beings seem too big for us to forgive. Holocaust survivor Simon Wiesenthal wrote a book called *The Sunflower: On the Possibilities and Limits of Forgiveness*. He shares a story from his time in the war and discusses whether forgiveness is possible. Then he asks a wide variety of writers to respond to the same question. It's a poignant and heart-wrenching book that contains no easy answers.

And yet, people and communities slowly recover from war, even as they bear scars that never disappear. Some people are able to experience forgiveness in their hearts in remarkable ways. I recently reread a book I first picked up as a teenager, *The Hiding Place*, by Corrie ten Boom. She learned to walk away from the people who harmed her in a prison camp and not hate them, even though her sister Betsie and many others were murdered there. She credited this ability to forgive entirely to the power of God in her life. In *The*

Hiding Place, ten Boom quotes her sister Betsie: "There is no pit so deep that [God's] love is not deeper still."[23]

> **PRAY**: *God, we want the end of the story*
>   *to contain forgiveness.*
> *But the story as we are living it now*
>   *is so far removed from that place,*
>   *we don't see how we can get from here to there.*
> *Alpha and Omega, you are the beginning and the end,*
>   *be our guide;*
>   *we trust in you. Amen.*

FOR REFLECTION

Fostering the conditions for forgiveness is important if we want to see it happen. Have you thought about forgiveness this way before? Does the metaphor of building steps to help people climb over a wall of sin make sense to you? Can you think of a specific situation where you might be able to foster forgiveness?

SATURDAY

Reaching Out

So when you are offering your gift at the altar, if you remember that your brother or sister has something against you, leave your gift there before the altar and go; first be reconciled to your brother or sister, and then come and offer your gift. —Matthew 5:23–24

READ: Matthew 5:21–26

This instruction from Jesus is so straightforward, you might think Christians would be really good at dealing with sin right away and not holding grudges. Sadly, that is not the case.

The church I attend was established in the early 1800s in southern Ontario; it has undergone three major splits in its history, showing that we have not taken these words to heart. I'd like to share about two of them.

The first split happened because some people wanted the church to change. An evangelical reform movement was sweeping through North America. It blew into our area in the 1840s when preachers from the United States came and taught about the importance of individual salvation and living a more Spirit-filled life. Newly energized Christians began thinking in fresh ways; some of them wanted to hold prayer meetings during the week in their homes.

This all sounds like a good thing; the Spirit moving, God renewing the church—who could take offense at that? But some in the church resisted the change; leaders were suspicious of members holding a prayer service without the main minister present. By 1848, the congregation was bitterly divided. Leaders had to decide whether these new evangelical ideas with their more emotional tone should be tolerated, or whether the old pattern of faith was better.

Both sides thought the other side was not truly Christian. The group that wanted to hold private prayer meetings accused the other side of not believing in the power of prayer. The other side called on the bishop and had the leader of the renewal movement officially silenced.

Things went from bad to worse, and eventually there were two congregations worshiping in two buildings. There were deep hurts on both sides, with families divided and friends not talking to one another. The church's witness in the area was tarnished, as the wider community knew these Christians could not get along with one another. The place that should have taught about forgiveness was torn apart by hatred.

Numerous factors led to this church split. Many people simply didn't like the church leader who led the reform movement. He had always been difficult to get along with, so when he began leading this reform, there was a tendency to think negatively about anything he did. He didn't help matters by stirring up others' anger with fiery, condemning speeches.

This church split also had to do with scripture. I think both groups put these words of Jesus uppermost: "And if your right hand causes you to sin, cut it off and throw it away; it is better for you to lose one of your members than for your whole body to go into hell" (Matthew 5:30). Each side wanted a "pure" church, and these verses about casting out were justification to exclude the offending members. Church members entirely disregarded today's scripture from Matthew about apologizing to those we've harmed before we participate in worship.

Tragically, forty years later in 1880, my home congregation split again. In an ironic twist, the group that had bitterly opposed prayer meetings had by this time adopted them, as well as the new practice of holding children's Sunday school. But some in the church were not happy with either innovation and wanted to return to the way things used to be. This time the church split was more dramatic, since both sides refused to leave the church property. So one group erected another building on the other side of the church cemetery. The two churches that couldn't get along were just a stone's throw apart, within singing distance of each other! (Within a generation, the church that left dwindled to a few members, and eventually closed.)

During both of these splits, at any point before a Sunday service, someone could have reached out and risked making a confession: "I'm sorry; I have hated you in my heart." Or maybe: "I have been so proud and so sure that my own interpretation of scripture was best. I'm sorry." Yet no apologies were spoken.

A century later, when I attended this congregation, we had a minister who always paid careful attention to his relationships. Over the years, he apologized to me for three separate things. In each case, it was about minor comments he made that I might have taken the wrong way. He was calling to make sure there were no hurt feelings—in each case, there weren't. My pastor's careful attention to keeping relationships on an even keel, and his humility in being able to apologize, was very much appreciated by our congregation. His example influenced my own actions when I became a pastor in that same congregation.

I remember a church member being angry with me for something I failed to do as their pastor. When I found out about this from a third party, I responded defensively at first, making excuses about why I didn't do that thing. But I remembered the model of my former pastor, and his example helped me find the humility to reach out and apologize instead of arguing my position.

Our congregation has survived for two hundred years. We can anticipate that the Spirit will bring big changes in the coming years. How will we react the next time we have a thorny conflict? Our history reminds us to listen especially carefully to the people with whom we disagree, because God speaks to all of us. Instead of separating when we disagree, we can reach out in love and hope.

> **PRAY:** *God, we confess your church is riddled with divisions.*
> *We have judged each other harshly, said bad things,*
>   *and missed the golden opportunity to listen.*
> *We've read your holy book with eyes open*
>   *only for words that support our own position.*
> *Help us respond to hurt with humility;*
>   *keep pride far from us.*
> *You will give us ears to hear,*
>   *and tongues to speak wise words*
>   *in times of church conflict. Amen.*

FOR REFLECTION

Think about a church or organization you know that has experienced a serious conflict. What are the issues? What scripture do you think is uppermost in their minds as they work through this conflict? In this situation, do you know if any apologies have been said? Why do you think it can be so hard for parties to apologize in church conflicts?

Making Peace

As he came near and saw the city, he wept over it, saying, "If you, even you, had only recognized on this day the things that make for peace! But now they are hidden from your eyes." —Luke 19:41–42

READ: Luke 19:29–44

There are three times described in Scripture where Jesus weeps or is deeply grieved. One time is at the tomb of Lazarus, his friend (John 11:35). The other is in the garden of Gethsemane as he prepares for his death on the cross (Matthew 26:37). And there is the time we read about today, when Jesus looks at the city of Jerusalem, and weeps over it. Jesus was moved to grieve for his friend, for himself, and for his city.

The timing seems odd for Jesus to cry as he looks over toward Jerusalem. The disciples have just been praising God with joyful loud voices, and the crowds are proclaiming that Jesus is king (Luke 19:37–38). Shouldn't this be a high point for Jesus? But Jesus is looking at the larger picture: the people do not recognize the things that make for peace.

Those followers who joined in the Palm Sunday parade likely had a lot of different ideas about how Jesus might bring peace. Perhaps they expected Jesus to march right up to the temple and be crowned king, thus ending Roman rule. Or perhaps they thought he would take over from the religious leaders who were seen as corrupt. Certainly some followers thought that if Jesus would just keep doing miracles, all would be well. The people wanted to see something amazing.

But Jesus' way of peace was different. The way of peace was not about seizing power from the religious authorities or from Rome. Rather, it was about bringing in the reign of God—ushering in a world order that involved love, self-sacrifice, and the willingness to suffer rather than do harm. Jesus' way of peace led not to a royal throne, but to a lonely hill outside the city. It led not to a golden crown, but to a crown of thorns.

The disciples, the rest of Jesus' followers, and all the crowd who had come out to meet him could not imagine what was in store for Jesus. Even worse, they desert him when he does not become the king they expect him to be. Jesus' words as he weeps prove to be true: "You did not recognize the time of your visitation from God" (Luke 19:44).

I traveled to Jerusalem twice, once in my early twenties and once in my fifties. On my first visit, I thought it was the most conflicted place I had ever visited. It was certainly the most militarized, with soldiers carrying big guns everywhere. I remember being shocked by soldiers at the beach wearing only swimming trunks and guns slung over their shoulders.

When I returned to Jerusalem thirty years later, things were much worse. The giant wall dividing Israel and Palestine had been constructed, and there were even more settlements (Jewish neighborhoods built on expropriated Palestinian land). There were more soldiers posted everywhere than last time. The Palestinians I talked to were persevering under restrictions and threats, but they shook their heads when they described how much harder life was.

On my most recent trip, I stayed in the home of a Christian Palestinian family in Bethlehem. From their back garden, we could look over the valley to Jerusalem in the distance. I commented on the beauty of the city on its hill. With great sadness the woman said that she had not been in Jerusalem for twenty years. Her repeated requests to visit the Holy City were denied, and without a permit she was unable to cross the checkpoint in the separation wall that divided the country. As a white foreigner, I could easily cross, and was intending to be at the Church of the Holy Sepulchre the very next day. But my host was denied, even though these were her holy places in her own homeland, where her ancestors had lived for millennia.

When we were in the northern part of Israel on that same trip, we stayed with a Jewish family who ran a guesthouse. I noticed when I went into my room that it had the strangest door—it was a foot thick! It turned out I was sleeping in a bomb shelter, with huge concrete walls and a door that locked with iron bars. The threat of attack was so real that some people lived with this sort of protection in place.

How can people find a way to peace in this situation? Neither side wants to admit to the harm they have caused, so there is little accountability. Each side blames the other for their own atrocities, claiming they were only acting in response to the other's violence. Jesus continues to weep over Jerusalem and other places around the world where violence and hatred rule. It is very easy to see where your opponent has gone wrong and needs to be held accountable. It is harder to think about our own accountability for our own actions, and harder still to find empathy for those who have harmed us.

Yet even in the most conflicted zones, people are working for peace. In Palestine and Israel there is an organization called The Parents Circle—Family Forum.[24] It consists of six hundred Israeli and Palestinian families who share something tragic in common. They all have lost a family member to this endless war, and they all want an end to conflict. They do everything they can to promote dialogue, tolerance, reconciliation, and peace.

Ordinary people are reaching out to work for peace, across walls, across great divides, across great evil done. They refuse to be enemies and instead have empathy for one another. God is working for peace in Jerusalem.

> **PRAY**: *Jesus, you came to show us the way to peace.*
> *Kingly, you took a towel*
> *and washed feet.*
> *With majesty, you served bread and wine.*
> *With honor, you prayed all night.*
> *With power, you wore chains.*
> *Jesus, remember us,*
> *when you come into your kingdom. Amen.*

FOR REFLECTION

The story of Jesus weeping over Jerusalem is so poignant. Do you weep over a city or community you know that "does not know the things that make for peace"? Where do you see God working for peace?

MONDAY

Relinquishing Revenge

I will make a way in the wilderness and rivers in the desert. —Isaiah 43:19

READ: Isaiah 43:16–21

The wilderness Isaiah knew was a barren and hot desert that received only a minimal amount of rainfall. Years ago I traveled to the wilderness around the Dead Sea: it was the hottest place I have ever visited. When we stepped off the bus in the parking lot near the sea, I felt slammed by the heat. I thought to myself, "I could die here, it's so hot!"

To add to the danger, we were standing near a beautiful turquoise lake shimmering in the sun. We were drawn to the water. But the water in the Dead Sea is so saline it feels oily, and it is very warm. A few gulps of this water could kill you. There was no hope that the water could sustain life—it was indeed a dead sea.

It is in this part of the world, where life survives on the edge if it survives at all, that the prophet Isaiah sets his vision. He describes God making rivers in this wilderness, God making water bubble up and flow, and God delivering people from thirst. God's salvation coming in surprising and powerful ways.

When we have been hurt terribly by someone, we can feel like we are in the wilderness without a hat or a map. Will we survive, or will we be consumed by the fire of rage inside us toward the person or group that hurt us? Will we find our way out of this wasteland of deep pain to a place of sanctuary again?

Robert inherited a solid family business when his parents died. In good faith, he welcomed an old friend into partnership in the business, expanding into some new areas. Over the next few years, things did not go well, and calamity fell upon them. Creditors wanted their money. When the company declared bankruptcy, it became apparent that Robert's so-called friend had enriched himself from the company, protecting his own assets, while Robert had been making sacrifices and giving 150 percent. His "friend" walked away from bankruptcy relatively unscathed while Robert lost the business and his livelihood.

The betrayal Robert felt was the biggest he had experienced in his life, and the bitterest part was that his family was suffering from it. With such a reduced income, their lifestyle changed substantially. Robert had hoped to welcome his children into the family business one day as he had been welcomed. Now he had nothing except an abiding and deep hatred for his former friend.

At first Robert had fantasized about revenge. He could picture himself confronting his former friend and punching him in the face. He imagined schemes where his former friend would lose all he owned. Then he imagined God exacting justice; maybe his former friend would have an accident or get sick.

Over time, he felt God calling him to sacrifice his revenge fantasies and let them go. Maintaining those fantasies was exhausting; he just wanted the pain and hurt to go away. Robert didn't want to talk to his friend who had expressed no remorse. He wanted most of all to not think about the person who caused the pain every single day of his life.

When great harm is done to us, it is as if giant chains are forged that connect us to the person who hurt us. The person who harmed us may not feel them, and may not think twice about what they've done. But for the victim, the restrictive chains are made of steel.

These chains binding Robert to his ex-partner were Robert's wilderness journey. He found it hard to go to church because the strong emotions he was feeling seemed out of place in worship. He talked to his pastor, who encouraged him to forgive his ex-partner, but Robert had no idea how to make that happen.

There were also other reasons he was having difficulty in church. Robert had never noticed before that the congregation he attended was filled with people from the same economic class. But now that his finances were in such terrible shape, he had a different vantage point. The church retreat was being held at a nice resort and participants had to pay their own way. Robert needed a retreat, but there was no way he could afford to take his family there. They were priced out of communal fellowship.

Members of their small group said, "Let us take you out to dinner." Robert felt this was a kind gesture because they knew about his financial woes. He and his wife hadn't been able to afford to eat out in months, but when the check came, no one picked up his bill, and he was left paying for a dinner he could not afford.

Now that Robert was sensitized to financial hardship, he saw other assumptions that his upper-middle-class church made in terms of what people wore, the vacations they could afford, the homes they owned, and even how they made decisions about the church building. Eventually, Robert and his family switched to attending an urban church, where they worshiped alongside people on social assistance or who had low incomes as well as people in the middle class.

In this congregation, Robert experienced the generosity of people who live in poverty. Some lived with almost nothing (and Robert felt rich in comparison), yet they were so willing to share what they had. This openheartedness moved Robert profoundly. Many of these people had also faced financial disaster, and some of them more than once. Slowly, Robert felt the hatred in his life being replaced by a feeling of gratitude for the people around him. He could relinquish his desire for revenge. This congregation was a stream of living water in the wilderness.

PRAY: *God of grace,*
thank you for all you provide
when we most need it,
in ways we least expect it.
You transform our parched places,
leading us away from the dead end of revenge.
You bring us into community,
where we find hope.
We are changed, refreshed, and renewed,
against all odds. Amen.

FOR REFLECTION

Have you ever felt chains connecting you to someone who has harmed you? If not, do you know someone who has? How has God helped to loosen or even eliminate those bonds? If you are just at the beginning of this process, what are your hopes and fears related to relinquishing revenge?

TUESDAY

Tending Sheep, Feeding Lambs

"Simon son of John, do you love me more than these?" He said to him, "Yes, Lord; you know that I love you." Jesus said to him, "Feed my lambs." —John 21:15

READ: John 21:15–19

This story takes place after Jesus has risen from the dead. It is the only conversation we have between Jesus and Peter post-resurrection. Peter's threefold denial is the awkward background that informs this whole conversation.

Logically, you would think what should come here is a confession—Peter should throw himself on the ground, saying, "I am so sorry I denied you." But Peter and Jesus skip that step. Can Jesus see the remorse on Peter's face and in his body language? Or does he simply know his friend so well that he can see how Peter is consumed with guilt?

Instead of waiting for Peter to act, Jesus asks Peter three times whether he loves him, and each time Peter assures Jesus that he does. Jesus gives him two tasks: "tend my sheep" and "feed my lambs." Peter will be given the opportunity to show whether he is a follower of Jesus by loving Jesus' flock.

Are we followers of Jesus? This is the primary question for Christians who have sinned and carry a burden of guilt, or for Christians who have been harmed and carry hatred. If we are followers of

Jesus, then we know what direction we are headed. We must always, first and foremost, "tend my sheep," and "feed my lambs." Love is our watchword.

In churches across Canada and the United States, one of the most divisive issues currently is whether LGBTQ+ people will be included in the church. This is not just a theoretical issue that theologians debate or church denominations ponder; it is a life-and-death issue for countless LGBTQ+ people.

When I was pastoring a congregation, a person who had recently moved to our city contacted me looking for a church home. She asked, "What is your congregation's attitude toward LGBTQ+ people?" She told me her story. For eight years she had attended a congregation, and then she went to a Gay Pride Parade to support a friend and posted a photo of the event on social media. Shortly afterward she was called into the church office and informed she could no longer sit on any committees or teach Sunday school. They said they would tolerate her attending church, but she really needed to change her beliefs if she wanted to stay.

She did not stay. She was struck by how the congregation was not at all interested in asking about her experience or beliefs or how she read scripture. They only wanted her to do exactly what they said.

"So that's why I need to know about this church," she told me. "I want to be sure that I will not be excluded because I support my LGBTQ+ friends. I don't think I could handle another experience of rejection like that." She added, "I have looked on your website, and I haven't seen anything about your position on this, so I need to know."

Our church had talked about being an affirming church, but so far nothing had been posted on the website. Many in the church were committed to including LGBTQ+ people and were eager to make a public statement. Others said, "Why do we have to make a big deal of it? Why can't gay or lesbian people just come and get to know us? Then they'll see how we are very welcoming."

Tellingly, I heard some fears from church members that if we put a welcoming statement on our website, then all sorts of LGBTQ+ people might start to attend and we would become "a one-issue church." The underlying assumption was that we could tolerate a few queer people, but not a lot of them. Some straight people were uncomfortable with the idea of having "too many" queer people in one place.

Our congregation was at the beginning of a learning journey about how queer people have been treated in the church. For most of history, LGBTQ+ people were cast out of the church. In more recent years, as being queer has become more acceptable in society, some churches have become welcoming, and other churches have doubled down on rejection.

I have heard people say, "We love the people but hate the sin." I do not believe they have listened to how that statement lands with LGBTQ+ people. If a church said to a straight couple, "We love you, but your marriage is sinful. You need to break up with your partner, and change your sexuality," it would not feel very loving. It would feel impossible.

Recently at a Christian college near my home, a queer student died by suicide. In a note they left behind, they specifically named the despair they felt because of a lack of support and acceptance for queer students at that college. Telling someone there is no place for them in the body of Christ is a life-and-death issue for many.

What does "tend my sheep" mean in regard to LGBTQ+ people? It means acknowledging the historical harm that has been done and listening to the hurt that people have experienced and are experiencing at the hands of the church. It means apologizing for harms done instead of sweeping the past under the rug as if nothing happened. The past must be remembered and lamented so that it is not repeated.

Most importantly, "feed my lambs" means acting lovingly going forward. Not just loving others according to the way straight people see the world, but loving from the perspective of LGBTQ+ people. There are many places in our society where homophobia endangers lives and human rights are compromised; the church can be a strong advocate for safety and justice.

> **PRAY:** *Thank you, God, that not all your lambs are just like me.*
> *Thank you for diversity in the church,*
> > *and the way your rainbow world*
> > *enriches life every day.*
> *Melt our frozen hearts*
> > *and fill them with repentance*
> > *for the way we've hurt individuals and communities*
> > *through bias and hatred.*
> *Open new pathways to dialogue,*
> > *and generous avenues of love. Amen.*

FOR REFLECTION

Followers of Jesus are meant to aim toward love in all they do and say. What would it look like to do this with someone you struggle to love? What are your next steps? Do you know of churches that are wrestling with inclusion or welcome of LGBTQ+ people? In what ways have you seen love missing from or entering those conversations?

TREADING
HOLY GROUND

Kneeling Faithfully

For I have set you an example, that you also should do as I have done to you. —John 13:15

READ: John 13:1–15

What was on Jesus' mind as he stooped to wash the feet of his followers? He already knew that he was about to be arrested and killed. He had only a few hours left on earth to imprint the most important lessons. Humble service is something Jesus wants us to learn by heart.

The only place that Jesus says "I have set you an example" is when he washes his disciples' feet. Because he was so specific in saying that, footwashing became a regular practice in the early church, usually celebrated before communion. This ritual is still present in some denominations today.

In the Catholic Church, on Maundy Thursday every year, the pope washes the feet of twelve people during mass. Bishops in the Lutherans and Methodist traditions wash the feet of those who are being ordained. In some Mennonite, Baptist, and Pentecostal churches, footwashing is a ritual that involves members washing each other's feet.

I have participated in footwashing services, and I have noticed there is always an element of awkwardness to this ritual. You can see it in the participants' body language as we stoop and wash and dry. It's there as we sit and have someone wash our feet. It's a humbling thing both to do for someone and to have done to you.

Adriaan Vlok was the minister of law and order in South Africa from 1986 to 1991, during the height of apartheid. Apartheid was a government system of racial segregation that discriminated against Black people and other people of color on the basis of race, primarily benefiting British South Africans and Afrikaners (white South Africans of Dutch descent). Under Vlok's leadership, his department assassinated Black anti-apartheid leaders and imprisoned tens of thousands.

After apartheid collapsed, Vlok returned to civilian life, where he devoted himself to reading the Bible. He was especially drawn to Matthew 5:23–24, which as we discussed last week, is where Jesus says if you are at the altar and remember someone has something against you, go and be reconciled. Vlok became increasingly uncomfortable reading these verses. Then one day he realized he had work to do.

In 2006, Vlok went to the office of Reverend Frank Chikane, a member of the African National Congress, the political party now in power in South Africa. When Vlok was in politics, his department had tried unsuccessfully to murder Chikane. When the two men met, Vlok found he was tongue-tied and couldn't speak. But he knew this might happen, so he had come prepared. He took out his Bible. On the flyleaf he had printed, "I have sinned against the Lord and against you! Will you forgive me?" He then asked if he could wash Chikane's feet; Chikane agreed. Vlok took a basin from a bag he was carrying, reached for a glass of water on the desk, knelt down, and washed Chikane's feet. Both men cried together.

This was a pivotal moment in Vlok's life. When he knelt to wash Chikane's feet, he realized that he had to let go of the superiority he had always felt over Black people. This new realization meant he needed to approach all Black people with humility and love. Vlok went on to wash many other people's feet, including the mothers of young people who had been murdered in a deliberate bus crash.

Chikane invited Vlok to speak in his church. There Vlok said it had taken him twelve years to reach the decision to atone for his sins. "I had to rid myself of my own pride, my egotism and my selfishness," he said. He was worried about washing feet, and he thought that people would likely misunderstand what he was doing. But he felt called to do it, saying, "If Jesus could do this, I could do this."

This ritual of service made national news in South Africa and outside the country as well. Many Afrikaners were angry with Vlok. They felt he took on the role of a servant, which (in their minds) was not right for a white person to do. They did not want white people apologizing to Black people. He was roundly mocked by people in the press, who called him a "quivering dog" and a "traitor."[25]

Jesus was walking with Vlok as he confronted his own racism, as he tried to apologize for what he did, and as he began the process of wholesale change in his actions. Jesus was also walking closely with Chikane, who now was in a position of power in the government. Jesus had prepared Chikane's heart so that he was able to accept this gesture of apology and forgive the attempt on his life.

Jesus sets an example for us today. Humility is a difficult quality to cultivate. Can you think of someone you harbor hostility toward or someone you have hurt? Imagine kneeling before them and washing their feet. Even imagining this can reveal our discomfort. When we dislike people, there is often an element of superiority in our minds, and taking a servant stance toward them upends that way of thinking.

There is something very vulnerable about letting someone touch our bare feet or touching someone else's feet. We are human: we all get dirt on our feet as we walk on God's good earth. Serving each other by footwashing is an intimate task. There are feet that need to be washed in our communities. Jesus has set us an example. Will we take our kneeling places?

PRAY: *After a hero's welcome in Jerusalem,*
*   you gathered the disciples in an upper room.*
Whatever they expected to happen that night,
*   it didn't have anything to do with dirty feet.*
Their own, held in your hands.
You were their champion, their leader,
*   now on your knees, doing the work of a servant,*
*   speaking to them of love.*
They went, clean footed, to the garden,
*   where you would be arrested and led away in chains.*
Jesus, lover of our souls and bodies,
*   teach us your way of humility. Amen.*

FOR REFLECTION

Have you ever participated in a footwashing ritual? What was it like to imitate Jesus' actions and to have your own feet washed like the disciples' feet? When you imagine washing the feet of someone whom you've hurt, what thoughts fill your mind and what emotions stir in your heart?

MAUNDY THURSDAY

Telling Our Stories

Jesus said to him, "Friend, do what you are here to do." Then they came and laid hands on Jesus and arrested him. —Matthew 26:50

READ: Matthew 26:6–9; John 12:1–6

The disciples were shocked when Jesus said, "One of you will betray me." Judas's story is told in different ways in the Gospels, giving us some insight into how the disciples and gospel writers came to terms with the betrayal of Judas.

In John's gospel, Judas is mentioned five times, and every single time the writer mentions that Judas is the one who betrayed Jesus. This gospel writer tells us that Satan "entered into" Judas (John 13:27). And we are told that when the woman pours the ointment on Jesus' feet, it is Judas who says this could have been sold for three hundred denarii. John's gospel names Judas as a thief who only wanted the money for himself.

In Matthew's gospel, we hear the same story of the woman pouring the ointment, but Matthew doesn't single out Judas as objecting to the act. Matthew recounts that all the disciples said it was wasteful to use the ointment. Matthew does not name Judas as a thief. I wonder about this. Perhaps Matthew as a former tax collector had some personal understanding of Judas's love of money. He decided not to name that in his story.

Matthew also adds a few important details to the story of Judas. Matthew remembers that in the garden of Gethsemane, Jesus calls Judas "friend." Significantly, Matthew also tells us that before Judas died, he repented of betraying Jesus and gave back the thirty pieces of silver (Matthew 27:3–6). John's gospel does not include that story, although he must have known it.

What's happening here? Matthew and John were both equally affected by the betrayal of Judas, but Matthew paints a kinder picture. He says Judas betrayed Jesus, but he tells the story in a more merciful way than John's gospel. Neither gospel suggests that Judas be forgiven for his betrayal, but I think Matthew was taking some steps along that road.

I wrote earlier about Evan, from a congregation I pastored. Evan was arrested after being caught sexually abusing a boy in our neighborhood. Evan was released on bail awaiting trial; his only restriction was not being near the boy he abused. Evan wanted to attend our church, and we worked on how that could happen safely. He was always accompanied by a volunteer who never left his side.

The first time Evan was in church after his arrest, it was communion Sunday. I was officiating. As people came up to gather in groups around the altar table for communion, I saw Evan at the back, and I thought, "Don't come up for communion! Don't come!"

But sure enough, Evan came up for communion. I found myself having a fierce conversation in my head with God about whether I should serve this man. I stormed inwardly, "God, he doesn't deserve to be here!"

When I heard myself saying those words in my head, it was like something very heavy dropped on my foot. I could not ignore what I said—it was sharp and painful. *Deserve* communion? Who among us deserves to be at this table?

My deepest presuppositions about the communion table were suddenly revealed. Somehow I felt I deserved to have the Lord's Supper because I did good things. Evan had done bad things, and I didn't think he qualified. This realization came to me in a flash, and I knew my thinking was wrong and needed to change.

We are loved simply because we are God's children. We don't earn God's love. At the Last Supper, Jesus broke bread and served all his disciples with love, even though he knew that Judas would betray him, and Peter would deny him. The communion table in our church belongs to Jesus, and not to us. As Evan stood in the circle waiting to be served, I prayed that God would give me grace to grow into the ministerial shoes I was wearing. I came away from the communion table changed, unburdened of a theology that was distorted and corrupting.

The following months were challenging. Our church accompanied Evan to court, where we listened to the testimony of the boy he abused. The boy and his parents sat on one side of the courtroom with friends and supporters, and we sat on the other. I had a son at home the same age as this boy who was testifying. I wanted so badly to be on the boy's side of the courtroom. But I knew that as Evan's pastor, I was called to support him. We spoke with the boy's family, who had known Evan from the time he was young. This family knew we had deep feelings of support for their son, but they wanted Evan to have some support too.

Evan eventually pled guilty, and received a suspended sentence. A few months later he died of a heart attack. At his funeral, someone from our congregation said, "We tried to support Evan. We didn't do that perfectly, but he knew we were trying."

Those events took place twenty years ago, and I am still unpacking what happened over those months. I have slowly found the words to tell that story and what it means to me.

Like the writers of the gospel of Matthew and John, we can choose how to tell our stories. When you think back to conflicts and hurts in your life, how do you explain what happened? Telling our stories through the lens of the Last Supper, we can see more clearly what needs to be seen.

PRAY: *With basins and bread and wine that night,*
you told your story of love.
We are still listening,
still trying to absorb the meaning.
As we tell our own stories of betrayal,
tales of disappointment and heartache,
we want to follow your example.
Jesus, lover of us all, we want to join you
on your knees in the garden. Amen.

FOR REFLECTION

Do you have any empathy for Judas? Have you ever found yourself in a situation where you didn't want another person to experience communion or other parts of church life? What beliefs led to those thoughts? Did knowing someone else's story change your perspective?

GOOD FRIDAY

Breaking Free

Then Jesus said, "Father, forgive them, for they do not know what they are doing." —Luke 23:34

READ: Luke 23:18–34

Today is a holy day where we remember the death of Jesus Christ our Lord. His trial. His stripes from the whip. His conversation with Pilate. His experience of the crowds rejecting his release. His long walk to Golgotha with a cross on his back. His crucifixion. His suffering. His words on the cross. And his death. We remember a Savior who gave everything for us.

What do we make of Jesus' words from the cross? "Father, forgive them." Religious leaders in Jesus' time were uncomfortable with the way he spoke about forgiveness. They grumbled when he offered forgiveness to a man who was paralyzed, because they thought only God should be allowed to forgive (Luke 5:17–26). Jesus also offered forgiveness to Zacchaeus: "Today salvation has come to this house" (Luke 19:1–10). In response, Zacchaeus pledges to live a new life.

On the cross, Jesus could have said, "Father, *I* forgive them, for they do not know what they are doing." He had forgiven the sins of other people, as we've just seen. Instead, Jesus asks God to forgive them. What is going on here?

An interpretation worth considering is that Jesus is giving this work to God to do because it was too much for him at the moment. Jesus was fully human as well as fully divine. Maybe he gives that forgiveness work to God because it is not humanly possible to forgive the very people who are torturing you when you are in pain and gasping for breath.

In real life, forgiveness sometimes seems impossible. We may not reach it, but we are called to move in that direction, even in small ways.

A person who has deeply influenced my understanding of forgiveness is Wilma Derksen, whose thirteen-year-old daughter Candace was murdered in Winnipeg, Manitoba, in 1984. Derksen has written several books about the aftermath of her daughter's murder. One of them is titled *This Mortal Coil*, in part because of the strong bond between the person who offended and Candace and her family. It's not a bond that Derksen's family chose, but it was thrust upon them. From the day that person murdered Candace, the murderer was present in the minds of the family wherever they went.

The Derksen family, because of their Christian faith, decided to pursue forgiveness. A headline in the local paper ran, "Derksens Refuse to Seek Revenge." But the person who had murdered Candace was faceless because there were no arrests in the investigation.

Twenty-two years went by and a cold-case investigation came up with a suspect, found through DNA evidence. Now the family had a name, Mark Edward Grant. Though he was not yet convicted, they knew he was connected through DNA evidence to the crime scene. As Wilma Derksen waited for the trial to begin, she read scripture, and the words "Love your enemies, and pray for them" stood out. She took the verse literally, and her family started praying for Grant by name.

In another book titled *Letting Go: One Woman's Walk to Forgiveness*, Derksen describes herself as a "determined but reluctant forgiver who needs a lot of time."[26] She is frank about her desire for revenge and fantasies for violence, the longing to hurt the one who hurt her child. Yet she is also clear about her identity as a Christian.

Forgiveness, for Derksen, never meant letting the perpetrator go free. Accountability was key. She longed to hear a confession from

Grant, which she did not receive. As they sat in the courtroom with Grant, she realized how important truth and justice were as companions to forgiveness. They could not be separated. Ultimately, Grant was acquitted on appeal, as the DNA evidence was determined to be flawed.

Derksen's writings communicate clearly that forgiveness is a wild journey, a lifelong, grueling uphill challenge that we are committed to because we are followers of Jesus, who took that uphill road before us. We cannot forgive completely like God forgives, but we work toward that goal. The road to forgiveness is a path to freedom, to breaking the mortal coil that joins us with those who harmed us.

Many of us will not face the challenge of forgiving the murder of our child, but the principles Derksen writes about hold true, even on smaller scales. We can experience different small injustices, and we may harbor feelings of anger toward many people. Many small chains still have the power to bind us.

Jesus comes alongside us in our many, various situations. Day by day, Jesus can help us break the links of the chains that bind us to the person or people who harmed us. We also can pray, "Jesus, you forgive them."

For those of us who have harmed others, the forgiveness demonstrated on Good Friday also provides us a path to freedom. Through Jesus, we know that God's love for us is complete, and that when we repent, God welcomes us with open arms. Knowing that God loves us does not immediately erase our own self-doubt or self-loathing; forgiveness from those we harmed may be entirely elusive. But we can live our lives in the comforting shadow of the cross. We can walk that path that Jesus walked, the path of self-sacrifice and commitment. We can break free using every day to work out our repentance and to strive for repair in whatever ways we can.

PRAY: *We come gingerly to prayer on this Good Friday,*
*   holding the pieces of our broken world.*
So much is ruined and spoiled,
*   so much hatred and anger,*
*   so many acts of violence.*
Our eyes turn to the cross
*   as evidence of our sinfulness—*
*   we crucified even the one who loved us most and best.*
Hear our prayers for all who long to forgive
*   but are mired in hatred and revenge.*
Hear our prayers for all who long to be forgiven
*   but are stuck in self-loathing and shame.*
You hold the keys to these prison doors, Jesus.
Our comfort lies in your words spoken at death's door:
"Father, forgive them, for they do not know what they
*   are doing,"*
*   and "Today you will be with me in paradise." Amen.*

FOR REFLECTION

Have you committed sins and not understood the full impact of the consequences? On this Good Friday, consider what the words "Father, forgive them, for they do not know what they are doing" might mean in your life. Consider writing a psalm of thanks to Jesus for his sacrifice for you.

HOLY SATURDAY

Embracing Love

When Jesus had received the wine, he said, "It is finished." Then he bowed his head and gave up his spirit. —John 19:30

READ: John 19:25–30

Jesus was crucified on Friday, the day before the Jewish Sabbath, and he rose from the dead on Sunday, the first day of the week. In the Christian tradition, the day between Good Friday and Easter Sunday is called Holy Saturday.

That name doesn't seem to fit if you think about what the disciples were experiencing that day. The Savior they followed for three years had just been tortured and murdered. For the followers who stood at the foot of the cross and witnessed his pain, the trauma would stay with them forever.

Jesus' final words, "It is finished," must have echoed in their minds. The hopes for the Messiah—dashed. The excitement of feeling the nearness of the kingdom of God—finished. Their beloved friend was dead. There was no life in his body anymore. They saw him being pulled down off the cross and taken away to a tomb. For the disciples who lived through it, they would never have called it holy.

But the holiness of that Saturday is that all is not what it seemed. The words that Jesus spoke were not a despairing cry for the end of everything, not the thud of a big book closing. Rather, it was the end of a chapter where Jesus in bodily form showed us the endless love of God. It was a love that we could not extinguish even though we killed him. The page turns for the disciples on Easter Sunday.

Jesus said to one of the people crucified with him, "Truly I tell you, today you will be with me in paradise" (Luke 23:43). Here on earth Jesus' dead body was in the tomb, but his spirit was alive with God. Holy Saturday is the time when all is lost and yet all is found. Holy Saturday is a day that is mysterious to Christians even now.

Julian lived in the little town of Norwich in England from 1342 to 1416. She was an anchoress, which means she dedicated her life to God by going into a room attached to a church and never leaving it again, in order to devote herself to prayer. To become an anchoress there was a ritual in the church very much like a funeral, because this woman was dying to the world. As an anchoress, Julian was an important part of the community. She participated in services through a window into the church, and she received many visitors who turned to her for advice. They would ask this holy woman to pray for them.

Norwich was a bustling city in the 1300s and the second largest city in England. The Black Death (also known as the bubonic plague) raced through Norwich when Julian was six years old, killing as much as half of the population. It continued to return cyclically every five to ten years, claiming more lives. Even more suffering piled on as the violence of the Peasants' Revolt raged through Norwich when Julian was thirty-nine years old.

Amid such massive turmoil, people must have thought the end of the world was near. Certainly the artwork and theology of the time reflect a grim fascination with death and a belief that an angry God was punishing the world.

At exactly that time, God sent a series of visions to Julian. In contrast to the gloom and pessimism of her time, the message she received from God revealed how good the world was. "For I know well that heaven and earth and all creation are great, generous and beautiful and good," she wrote.[27] She was shown God's tender care for the world. "All will be well, and every kind of thing will be well."[28]

In one of her visions, Julian saw something in the palm of her hand. The item was round like a hazelnut. She asked God, "What can this be?" And God said, "It is all that is made." She wondered at how little it was, and vulnerable. God said, "It lasts and always will, because God loves it." Julian would later write, "In this little thing, I saw three properties. The first is that God made it, the second is that God loves it, the third is that God preserves it."[29]

The book where she recorded her visions is called *Revelations of Divine Love* or *Showings*. I reread it during the pandemic and was struck by the enduring relevancy of her visions for our times.

On this Holy Saturday, as you think about the world, are you hopeful? Many people, including me, can sometimes barely watch the news. We live with a sense of dread that the world is going from bad to worse, and we all face calamity. The looming catastrophe of climate change, wars, economic inequality, racism, the danger of political instability: together these form into an overwhelming sense of hopelessness. This is compounded by our own personal tragedies of sins we have committed, sins done to us, and our ongoing challenges with giving and receiving forgiveness. We can easily feel that our lives are permanently crooked or warped.

But nothing that happens or that we cause to happen can change God's love for us. God is with us and will be with us, on this Holy Saturday and every day. All shall be well. God's resurrecting Spirit hovers over the deep, including over our deepest sorrows, fears, and mistakes, as individuals and as the human race.

PRAY: *On this Holy Saturday, God,*
we pray for strength in difficult times.
Our troubles are so heavy,

sometimes we feel buried under them;
weight upon weight presses us down in the dark.
Just when we fear this might be our tomb,
we hear the shock of Jesus' voice
calling us to come out.
We pause in the darkness,
wondering for the first time
whether what we are
is buried
or planted.

FOR REFLECTION

When you think about the state of the world, do you feel primarily optimistic or pessimistic? Do you find hope in the words God gave to Julian of Norwich? How does the presence of God's Spirit in the world affect how you think about the future?

EASTER SUNDAY

Leaping Over Walls!

But these words seemed to them an idle tale, and they did not believe them. —Luke 24:11

READ: Luke 24:1–12

Christ the Lord is risen today! Up from the grave he arose! Lift your glad voices! Today is Easter day! We join with the angels when we give thanks for the resurrection of Jesus Christ.

As we read resurrection accounts in the Gospels, we see the male disciples reacting to the women who were the first witnesses of the resurrection—it seemed to them "an idle tale" (Luke 24:11). It is so telling that skepticism permeated some of the first responses to the biggest news of our salvation. I wonder how it felt for the women to be disbelieved. Nevertheless, they persisted.

We are still skeptical people today, not sure that God can bring about resurrection in our own lives. When we face the biggest messes and the biggest sorrows, we think they are insurmountable problems that sentence us to suffering. But God is an impossibility specialist who surprises us with joy time and again.

When we have harmed someone, we can eventually be freed of the burden of guilt because of Jesus. We can devote ourselves to living as people forgiven by God even if there is no expression of human forgiveness. We can cultivate repentance, apologize, ask how to repair what we've done, and allow ourselves to be held accountable. We can ask for forgiveness from others, knowing that whether they grant it is not in our control.

When we are harmed, some of us follow Jesus by walking away and choosing not to hate someone. Through daily hard work we loose the chains that bind us. We try to let go of hatred and revenge. We set boundaries and cultivate a place of safety.

Others among us who are harmed aim toward restored relationships. We let go of the burden of self-blame. We try to nurture forgiveness, we wait for it to be born in us. We practice the discipline of kind thoughts.

All this work does not happen on a level playing field. Some of us may have more to forgive because we've experienced greater harm. Our capacity to forgive can become depleted. We need communities to support us and strengthen us on the way. Yet these communities and organizations are often on their own journeys of repentance, accountability, and forgiveness.

The challenge is that we are never only the sinned against. We are also sinners. Each one of us. We are people who are trying to forgive others, and simultaneously we are needing forgiveness from those we have harmed. We are all human.

In 2005, James Loney and three other men were kidnapped in a war zone in Iraq. These men were participating in what is now called Community Peacemaker Teams, a group that places trained peacemakers in conflict zones to engage in nonviolent interventions.

During the long days of captivity, their captors watched American action movies. One day, Loney recognized the movie they were watching, and he was surprised to notice the captors cheering for the heroes. Loney did a double take—he was sure his captors were the bad guys in the film and he was on the good side. He reflected on the idea that everyone tells their own story with themselves as the hero. It was just one of many little insights he had into the humanity of his captors, who had hopes and fears and vulnerabilities too.

Loney describes a spiritual exercise that Tom Fox, another member of his group, practiced during their imprisonment. Fox would hold a link of the chain in his handcuffs, picture in his mind a loved one or a captor, and then he would breathe. On the inhale he breathed in the suffering of that person, and on the exhale he breathed out healing and compassion toward them. He would do that for a cycle of four breaths, picturing that person surrounded by light, and then move on to another link, another person.[30]

Tom Fox was killed by the kidnappers, but Loney and the two other men were rescued. Loney reflects on the process of forgiveness, calling it an audacious leap of faith. He forgave his captors, writing: "May you be healed of your violence. May you be reborn to the knowledge of your forgiveness." He reflected, too, on the need for repentance and accountability in relationships between nations. There is so much sin in the world that needs to mended.

In the early church, Easter was a traditional day for baptism, the day where Christians remember that death cannot hold us. This is something we can reflect on today. In the Hebrew Bible, David offers a song of praise after God delivers him from his enemies. He talks about the waves of death encompassing him, then describes his rescue by God in a series of detailed images, and finally declares, "By my God I can leap over a wall" (see 2 Samuel 22:5–30). Resurrection miracles can happen when we pray for God to help us.

My hope for you is that you will become skilled at leaping over the walls of sin that separate us. I hope that forgiveness can grow in you for the people who have harmed you, and be born in good time through the grace of God. When you sin, I hope that repentance, repair and accountability will help you build steps for others up walls you have created. I hope that together we can create communities that are not afraid to name sin. Communities of compassion that can walk with both the injured and those who have done harm. Communities that have patience for all who are on lengthy repentance and forgiveness journeys. When we follow Jesus, little by little and along the way, we can drop the burdens that weigh us down.

Thank you for reading this book and taking this Lenten journey with me. May it give us great joy to know that, together, we can say, "Jesus, we trust in you."

> **PRAY:** *God of grace and love,*
> *from the depths of our tombs,*
> *you call us into your marvelous light and life,*
> *just as you called Jesus, the firstborn of the dead.*
> *Thank you for giving us the Bible,*
> *and a community in which to read it.*
> *Jesus, bearer of our burdens,*
> *thank you that you are God with us,*
> *never forsaking us, come what may.*
> *Journey with us as we repent of our sin,*
> *and seek to repair the harm we've done.*
> *Thank you for the gift of forgiveness,*
> *this complicated treasure.*
> *We will unpack it in a thousand actions*
> *and through it find freedom in the hardest places.*
> *Protect us from the temptation to misuse this gift,*
> *to wield forgiveness like a weapon, or minimize its complexity.*
> *Holy Spirit, we need your presence in our communities,*
> *inspiring us, uniting us, forming us.*
> *You rest upon us early and late,*
> *breathing hope upon us, like a benediction. Amen.*

FOR REFLECTION

Where is God inviting you to experience resurrection? How does being someone who is both sinned against and a sinner affect your ability to empathize with others? What insights about forgiveness have you gleaned over this Lenten season? Do you feel God calling you to work on forgiving someone or to foster conditions where you might be forgiven?

GUIDE FOR SMALL GROUPS

Consider gathering a group of friends or church members together to work through this devotional. Insights from a group can deepen your understanding of how forgiveness happens. Take time to read the Bible passages aloud together, perhaps using various biblical translations. Then share how you each interpret them. The Holy Spirit speaks to us through the lives of others; as we grapple with the challenges of forgiveness in different contexts, wisdom grows.

Gathering times: You may want to meet initially on Shrove Tuesday to get the group started, with participants then reading the devotionals for the week ahead. Or you could meet on Wednesdays at the end of each week of devotionals, concluding the Wednesday after Easter. If you are using this as a Sunday school discussion guide, start meeting the Sunday after Ash Wednesday, and reflect on the previous week's entries. If you have a big group, divide into smaller groups for discussion so that more people have a chance to share a relevant story.

Leading discussions: Our experiences with repentance, accountability, repair, and forgiveness are diverse. Expect to be surprised by what you hear. Importantly, I encourage you to treat this gathering as a sacred space, as people come with the offerings of their lives. Any story shared in the group should not be repeated outside the group without the permission of the one who shared it. Come with an open mind, with curiosity, and with questions. Try to leave "should" and "must" and "just" at the door.

As a leader, you set the tone. Be open and welcoming. Don't rush to fill silent spaces between people's comments. Sometimes insights grow best in the pauses. Demonstrate patient, active listening.

Feel free to pick and choose from and modify the questions for discussion, or add your own. Some of these questions echo those offered in the daily reflections. They are only *prompts* for discussion; you know what will work best in your group.

I hope that together you can be vulnerable with one another. Share joyful stories of forgiveness—they are gifts from God to be celebrated. Think carefully about what else you might want to share. I suspect that deep down, many of us harbor hatred toward someone, and we don't like to admit it or talk about it. Or we don't want to share how we have hurt others and desire forgiveness that we have not yet received. If we only tell our success stories, we set up unrealistic standards for forgiveness. It is hard to talk about the wilderness places where we find ourselves at square one in the forgiveness journey, but it's fruitful when we find a way to do so.

Sensitive topics: Tears may happen, and some stories may leave the storytellers or the group emotionally raw. Give people permission to take care of themselves in the form of leaving the meeting space and taking a break. Follow up with people who step out to ensure they have pastoral care. Begin the sessions by establishing group commitments to confidentiality and respectful listening so that participants can feel secure in a vulnerable space.

Prayers: A prayer is included with the daily reflections, and additional prayers are included in the pages that follow. Choose from among them to use at the beginning and end of each session. You may want to invite someone in the group to read the prayer, or you may ask all willing participants to read in unison. All the prayers included in this book are guidelines; feel free to add to them, or modify them, or to invite people in the group to pray extemporaneously instead. Especially when group members share painful stories, pause and pray for one another specifically.

I hope that your time exploring forgiveness together during Lent will be fruitful. May you draw closer to God and each other.

WEEK 1

Seeking Repentance

Ask each person to write down a sentence or two about what they've been taught that the Bible says about forgiveness. How central is the word *repentance* in these teachings?

Public calls to repentance are numerous in Scripture. How important are prayers of confession in worship services you attend? How specific are these prayers, and why are they important?

Think about a time when you realized you did something wrong, and describe the emotions that accompanied that realization.

Can you think of a time when an organization realized it had done something wrong? How did the leaders respond?

Making excuses for one's wrongdoing is a very human trait, starting with Adam in the garden of Eden. Can you think of a way you've made excuses? How did God help you take responsibility for your actions?

Think about a time when you felt sorrow or penitence about something you did. If you were raised in the Christian church, what were you taught about the process of forgiveness? Was forgiveness taught as being mostly between you and God, or were you taught there was a more outward element?

PRAY: *God, you great Searcher of our hearts,*
is this the place where remorse begins?
You know our lives through and through.

You've seen the wrongs we try to hide,
the wrongs we dare to do in plain sight,
and the wrongs we have totally forgotten.
As we pause in the awareness of your gaze on us,
is this the place where repentance begins?

(Pause for a time of silence.)

You know how we can right the wrongs we've done,
the words of apology that need to be spoken,
the old ways of living that must be abandoned.
As you reveal new, hopeful paths for us,
is this the place where redemption begins?
Thank you for Jesus, who knows exactly
how we are tempted
and how we can overcome temptation.
Through his life, death, and resurrection,
he ushered us into this place
where forgiveness finds us,
where forgiveness flows through us. Thank you! Amen.

PRAY: *God, our Hope, be our guide through all the terrains*
of sinfulness.
When sin is glittering, and we have eyes for nothing else,
be with us.
When sin is disguised, and we do wrong thinking it's right,
be with us.
When sin feels justified, and we know it's wrong
but still think it's OK for us,
be with us.

When sin is something we refuse to think about,
and we go our own way,
be with us.
When sin is crystal clear, and we overstep with conscious malice,
be with us.
When sin is foggy, and we abandon caution
and go full steam ahead,
be with us.
When we find ourselves mired in the muck of sinfulness,
stuck in the destruction we've caused,
be with us.
Jesus, hear our prayer of confession,
and show us a path to freedom.
Map out how to right the wrongs we've done.
Give us strength to turn from sin,
living in new ways, thinking new thoughts.
We want to live in the landscape of your grace forever. Amen.

WEEK 2

Addressing Sin

In your church community, is sin something that is talked about a lot, or only rarely? How do you react when people discuss sin?

Can you share an example of a time when you were called to repentance? Was it through a prayer, a sermon, a conversation with someone, or simply an inner conviction? Do you think your congregation does a good job calling people to repentance? Why or why not?

Do you know someone who has had to live their whole life with the consequences of someone else's sin? How might these long-term consequences affect that person's ability to work on forgiveness?

In your family, are there jagged endings to hurtful stories where no apologies were said and pain lingers? How do you see God walking with you in that experience?

Give an example of how a larger system can lead individuals to sin. Can you think of ways we might address that sin? How does focusing on individual sin alone create more problems?

Is polarization (an us-versus-them mentality) something you experience in your own community? Describe how that mentality formed and how it impacts relationships. Is God calling you to reach out over a dividing wall?

PRAY: *Gracious God, we confess our sins to you.*
Our hands and hearts are not clean.
We desire power and status
and neglect our duty as your servants.
We allow ourselves to become preoccupied
with things we own or want to own,
freely putting on the chains of consumerism.
Open our eyes to the way our lifestyles
affect and harm those both near and far away.
We turn away from all who are hungry and homeless,
thinking they are someone else's problem.
We show our worst side to those who care for us most.
Forgive us for sour faces and cold shoulders,
for clenched fists and icy stares.
You call us to carry a cross,
and we complain as soon as the way is hard.
We forget how much we have received
and how little we have sacrificed.
Remove our hearts of stone,
and give us hearts of flesh,
which beat to the rhythm of faith, hope,
and love—always love. Amen.

PRAY: *God, we come in prayer to you,*
burdened with our unhappy business;
all the deeds done under the sun
we would rather not remember,
the sounds of sin in our world.
The explosions caused by bombs made in our own factories.

The cries of the hungry who are not fed
*   in our own communities.*
Our own hurtful words hurled at those we love.
The echoing silence of creatures we have driven to extinction.
Hearer of all, you know too clearly the sorrows of our world!
Forgive us our sins, and help us, as much as we are able,
*   to right the wrongs we've done.*
Give us words of humble repentance
*   to share with those we've wronged,*
*   and ringing courage to stand up*
*   for the voiceless creatures of the world.*
We need a resounding love for the lowest and the least.
Most of all, tune our ears to the voice of Jesus
*   so that, always and everywhere, we can hear*
*   your song of peace for every creature under the sun. Amen.*

WEEK 3

Pursuing Freedom

Self-blame is common for people who have been harmed as children. How would hearing a strong emphasis on sin and unworthiness affect someone who already feels they are unlovable? How do you think the church can help support and free individuals who are affected by abuse?

Have you or has someone you know ever been betrayed or desperately hurt by a close friend or family member? What scars are carried from that experience? Has setting boundaries been a part of your faith journey to heal from the betrayal?

Can you think of someone whom you have forgiven numerous times? How did it feel to keep giving someone second, tenth, and twentieth chances? Have you ever seen forgiveness being misused, and in turn it not helping the situation?

Can you share an example of an apology you received? Was it helpful, or did it lack something?

Are there people you want an apology from who have never offered one?

If you have ever forgiven someone without receiving an apology from them, consider the circumstances. What enabled you to forgive anyway?

Have you seen the church doing the work of deliverance in someone's life? Perhaps your congregation has responded to a family experiencing domestic violence. Was the congregation able to help the family, or were there things that hindered the family from finding safety or healing?

Has someone demanded forgiveness from you when you weren't ready to give it?

PRAY: *God of grace,*
in this season of Lent,
we ask for four gifts.
Courage to admit the harm
we know we've done.
Insight to grasp the harm
we didn't know we committed.
Humility to apologize if we can
and to ask how to make things right.
And finally, wisdom
to do well the hard work of repair,
with a willing spirit and a kind heart.
It is through your freeing love we are saved. Amen.

In this prayer, you are invited to use your imagination and
picture things during a time of silence. You can close your
eyes if you wish. Rather than forming sentences in your mind,
just create a picture. These pictures will be our group's prayer.
Picture in your mind someone who has forgiven you for
something you did wrong. Imagine standing beside them and
feeling the freedom of that forgiveness.

(Allow twenty seconds of silence.)

*Picture in your mind someone who has hurt you. Picture
yourself standing far away from them. Imagine a third person
coming to stand between you—it's Jesus. Feel God's love
flowing from Jesus toward both of you.*

(Allow twenty seconds of silence.)

*Picture in your mind that same person who hurt you, now
standing alone. Picture yourself surrounded by a community
of people who are supporting you and keeping you safe. If
you are able, imagine sending kindness back to the person
who hurt you through your outstretched hand.*

(Allow twenty seconds of silence.)

In closing, you can offer these words:

*Spirit of infinite kindness,
your love reaches out across every divide.
It fills every need, it heals every wound, it satisfies every hunger.
We want your love to flow through us;
we are citizens in your kingdom of kindness. Amen.*

WEEK 4

Responding to Brokenness

Think of a time someone pointed out something you were doing wrong. Did you see that person as a prophet? How do we often respond to prophets who point out our sin?

Think of a system that causes a lot of harm in your community. Do you know anyone who is trying to challenge it? How could your church community come alongside the challenge efforts? What might hold you back from offering such support?

Are you nursing a deep wound that you find hard to forgive? Do you anticipate carrying this for the rest of your life? How is God inviting you to make small steps toward forgiveness?

Think of someone who caused harm, made apologies, and now wants to return to a former position of leadership or rejoin an intimate or family relationship. How can boundaries help protect that person from the temptation to sin again?

How do you discern when it is appropriate to confront another person who caused harm? If there is a power imbalance between the parties, how might the harm be addressed safely? How might a fear of conflict contribute to our unwillingness to confront someone who has hurt us or caused another person harm? How might your church community intervene and help in such situations?

Have you ever experienced a surprising twist in your life where God brought new life to a place you thought was dead and buried? Have you ever seen a broken relationship resurrected and restored?

Share about that experience and examine the power of God to change us.

Are there scorecards in your life where you keep accounts of who has hurt you and how much? Can you think of ways to abandon scorekeeping and adopt a generous attitude? Or perhaps you know someone has kept careful score of your slights. What would it mean to have those erased?

PRAY: *God of hope,*
 you know the hurt we carry;
 the pain from deep wounds—
 blows felt, cutting words received,
 the betrayal, the double cross,
 and the dull ache of neglect.
We juggle each memory,
 trying to shift the load.
But there's a haunting sense
 that we've reached our limit
 and this camel's back
 cannot take one straw more.
We need more strength, more energy,
 more wisdom to know how to cope.
Jesus, you walked a road to Jerusalem
 carrying a heavy load that you took up willingly,
 knowing it was yours alone to bear.
We hear your call to follow,
 and your offer of light burdens—
 we so long for this to be true.
God of the winding road,
God of the heavy load,

God of the time to pick things up,
God of the time to lay things down,
  be our God, now and always. Amen.

PRAY: *Even in the small schemes of our lives*
    there are times when we come upon the big mess
    that we may or may not have caused.
The challenges lobbed, first shots fired,
    volleys of words thrown like grenades,
    the bodies prone, the revenge promised.
War even on the tiniest scale wreaks havoc
    and rejects consolation through the years.
The fog of war never completely lifts,
    but the casualties are completely clear:
    trust and innocence blown to smithereens,
    hope mired in the trenches,
    with bitterness like a rat, gnawing on grudges.
Jesus, make it stop.
Give us new eyes to imagine relationships restored,
    forgiveness offered, and goodwill renewed.
Give us a vision of this battlefield transformed.
We long for a field of winter wheat,
    green after the fiercest season,
    friends embracing enemies and an armistice to the cold war—
    a white flag in the spring of peace.

WEEK 5

Building Forgiveness

Do you know anyone who was overthrown by God, sending them in an entirely different direction? If the person you are thinking about is you, reflect on how your life might be different now if God had not intervened.

Do you know anyone who has been pressured to forgive someone who was hurting them? How did the story turn out? Why do we feel compelled to try to force people into forgiveness?

Fostering conditions for forgiveness is important if we want to see it happen. Have you thought about forgiveness this way before? Does the metaphor of forgiveness being similar to taking steps up a wall make sense to you?

Think about a church or organization you know that is experiencing a serious conflict. What are the issues? What scripture do you think is uppermost in their minds as they work through this conflict? In this situation do you know whether or not any apologies have been said? Why do you think it can be so hard to speak apologies to others in church conflicts?

Like Jesus, do you weep over a city or community you know that "does not know the things that make for peace"? Where do you see God working for peace?

Have you ever felt giant chains connecting you to someone who has harmed you? If not, do you know someone who has felt that way? How has God helped to loosen those bonds? If you are just at the beginning of this process, what are your hopes and fears?

As victims carrying great pain, or as sinners who have caused harm, the ultimate question is still the same: "Are we followers of Jesus?" Why can it be so challenging to take the direction of kindness when we think of someone we struggle with?

Do you know of churches that are wrestling with inclusion or welcome of LGBTQ+ people in worship and leadership? In what ways have you seen love entering or exiting those conversations?

PRAY: *On Palm Sunday, we remember the crowd's response*
 as you entered into Jerusalem.
We admit that we, too, have paid lip service to you.
We shout, "Hosanna!" one minute
 and deny you the next.
You call us to love one another
 but we are burdened with the pain of the harm done to us;
 we think we can never put it down.
The words in our heads have often been
"Can't," "Won't," "Never," and "Impossible."
Believing our problems are too deep for you,
 we have underestimated your power
 and stewed in our misery.
We repent of this obstinacy.
God, in your mercy, hear our prayer.
We have received your forgiveness
 but have found it difficult to forgive others.
We hold grudges, we keep scores,
 we carefully tally every slight
 while ignoring the harms we ourselves inflict.
We keep our heads down and refuse to see
 the systems of injustice that ensnare us and our neighbors;

we claim our innocence while people suffer.
God, in your mercy, hear our prayer.
Gracious God, we long to be your dear disciples,
washing each other's feet, forgiven and forgiving.
We long to be faithful, awake with you in the darkest hour.
We long to follow in your footsteps,
even if they lead to a cross on a barren hillside.
These are the desires of our hearts.
God, in your mercy, hear our prayer.

PRAY: *Forgive the division and animosity we have fostered*
between different kinds of churches.
We're so sure our little branch is superior,
we look down our noses at a whole tree
teeming with varying practices and beliefs.
We are so convinced of our special place close to your heart.
Cast out all casting out; expel all expellings.
Open channels in us for your love to flow.
Give us dreams of new flowerings we do not control,
hosts of vibrant, diverse congregations
multiplying in uncountable ways,
each one a witness to your power, and not our own. Amen.

WEEK 6

Treading Holy Ground

Have you ever participated in a footwashing ritual in church? What was it like to imitate Jesus' actions or to have someone else wash your feet? If you imagine washing the feet of someone whom you've hurt, what goes through your mind and heart?

Do you have any empathy for Judas? Have you ever found yourself in a situation where you didn't want another person to participate in communion or experience other parts of church life? What beliefs led to those thoughts? What do you think after reading this week's devotions?

Consider what the words "Father, forgive them for they do not know what they are doing" mean in your life. Have you committed sins and not understood the full impact of the consequences? How does knowing about God's extensive forgiveness change you?

When you think about the state of the world, do you feel basically optimistic or pessimistic? Do the words God gave to Julian of Norwich offer you any hope? How does the presence of God's Spirit in the world affect how you think about the future?

Where is God calling you to experience resurrection? How does being both a sinner and someone who has been sinned against affect our ability to feel empathy for others?

As you reflect on this period of Lent, what insights have you gleaned about forgiveness? Do you feel God nudging you to work on forgiving someone or to foster conditions where you might be forgiven?

PRAY: *Jesus, you loved us in the beginning*
and you love us to the end.
Even on the night you were betrayed,
you took a towel, and washed others' feet.
We confess that we are reluctant to think of you
doing such a humble task, least of all for us.
Like Peter, we protest.
We fail to see how love takes the lowly way,
how it is worked out in a thousand small acts of kindness,
a thousand humilities.
For ourselves we prefer the grand gestures,
love that can be seen and applauded,
love that first and foremost makes us feel good.
You showed us a different way.
Jesus, Towel-Bearer, Foot-Washer, Cross-Carrier,
you have set us an example
for our own Good Friday journeys.
We want to follow you wherever you lead us. Amen.

PRAY: *God of life, thank you for empty tombs,*
and Jesus Christ, risen and alive.
Thank you that death does not have the final word, ever.
We pray for all who find it difficult to believe in resurrection,
all whose pain and sorrow weigh them down.
Show us how we can walk alongside them.
You bring life where there is lifelessness,
you resurrect hope where we feel only despair,
you fill us with energy when we are at our lowest ebb.

Thank you for working every day in every way,
  surprising us by calling out potential we didn't know we had.
You bring Easter to each of us, with joy and delight.
We want to meet you in the garden of our hearts,
  free and unburdened, saved by the One who created us.
We pray these things in the name of Christ,
  whose love surrounds us, now and forever. Amen.

Notes

1. Torah Bontrager, *Amish Girl in Manhattan: A Crime Memoir* (New York: Amish Heritage Press, 2021). See also her website, TorahBontrager.com.

2. Augustine, *The Confessions of St. Augustine,* translated by Edward B. Pusey (New York: Random House, 1949), 158.

3. Martin Luther, quoted in Roland Bainton, *Here I Stand: A Life of Martin Luther* (Nashville: Abingdon Press, 1950), 185.

4. John Paul Tasker, "Canada Reports Worst Wildfire Season on Record—and There's More to Come This Fall," CBC News, August 11, 2023, https://www.cbc.ca/news/politics/canada-wildfire-season-worst-ever-more-to-come-1.6934284.

5. Phyllis Trible, *Texts of Terror: Literary-Feminist Readings of Biblical Narratives* (Philadelphia: Fortress Press, 1984), 37–63.

6. For more information, check out @AuschwitzMuseum on social media.

7. For example, Government of Canada, "Factsheet—Anti-Semitism in Canada," February 22, 2023, https://www.canada.ca/en/canadian-heritage/corporate/transparency/open-government/standing-committee/ahmed-hussen-pch-contract-cmac/antisemitism-canada.html; and "Audit of Antisemitic Incidents 2022," Anti-Defamation League, https://www.adl.org/resources/report/audit-antisemitic-incidents-2022.

8. DeNeen L. Brown, "Lynchings in Mississippi Never Stopped," *Washington Post*, August 8, 2021, https://www.washingtonpost.com/nation/2021/08/08/modern-day-mississippi-lynchings/; *Report to the United Nations on Racial Disparities in the U.S. Criminal Justice System*, The Sentencing Project, April 19, 2018, https://www.sentencingproject.org/reports/report-to-the-united-nations-on-racial-disparities-in-the-u-s-criminal-justice-system/; Cheryl Thompson, "Fatal Police Shootings of Unarmed Black People Reveal Troubling Patterns," NPR, January 25, 2021, https://www.npr.org/2021/01/25/956177021/fatal-police-shootings-of-unarmed-black-people-reveal-troubling-patterns.

9. Aleksandr Solzhenitsyn, *The Gulag Archipelago 1918-1956: An Experiment in Literary Investigation*, III-IV, translated by Thomas P. Whitney, (New York: Harper & Row, Publishers, 1975), 615.

10. Hannah Arendt, *Eichmann in Jerusalem: A Report on the Banality of Evil* (London: Penguin Classics, 2022).

11. To learn more about Carrie Nation, see "Carry A. Nation," Historic Missourians, last modified December 22, 2022, https://historicmissourians.shsmo.org/carry-nation/.

12. Keith Humphreys et al., "Responding to the Opioid Crisis in North America and Beyond: Recommendation of the Stanford *Lancet* Commission," *The Lancet* 399, no. 10324 (February 2, 2022), https://www.thelancet.com/commissions/opioid-crisis.

13. See, e.g., Aaron Kessler, Elizabeth Cohen, and Katherine Grise, "The More Opioids Doctors Prescribe, the More Money They Make," CNN, March 11, 2018, https://edition.cnn.com/2018/03/11/health/prescription-opioid-payments-eprise/index.html.

14. Beverly Wildung Harrison, "The Power of Anger in the Work of Love: Christian Ethics for Women and Other Strangers," *Union Seminary Quarterly Review* 36 (1981): 41–57.

15. UN Office on Drugs and Crime, *Global Study on Homicide 2018: Gender-Related Killing of Women and Girls* (Vienna, UNDOC, 2018), 13, https://www.unodc.org/documents/data-and-analysis/GSH2018/GSH18_Gender-related_killing_of_women_and_girls.pdf.

16. Werner Fast, "The Story of My Family," *Conrad Grebel Review* 18, no. 2 (Spring 2000): 79–82.

17. William Shakespeare, *Julius Caesar*, act 3, scene 2.

18. See Allen Dwight Callahan, "Perspectives for a Study of African American Religion from the Valley of Dry Bones," *Nova Religio* 7, no. 1 (July 2003): 44–59.

19. Susan Clairmont, "Sex Offender Watch Group Gets Funding Reprieve," *Hamilton Spectator*, March 7, 2014, https://www.thespec.com/news/hamilton-region/2014/03/07/sex-offender-watch-group-gets-funding-reprieve.html. For more on Circles of Support and Accountability, see www.CoSACanada.org.

20. See Cornelia Dean, "Executive on a Mission: Saving the Planet," *New York Times*, May 22, 2007, https://www.nytimes.com/2007/05/22/science/earth/22ander.html; Joel Makower, "Why Aren't There More Ray Andersons?," GreenBiz, August 6, 2012, https://www.greenbiz.com/article/why-arent-there-more-ray-andersons.

21. Jean Vanier, the cofounder of L'Arche, was a friend of Henri Nouwen and encouraged him to come to L'Arche. Vanier died in 2019. A report published by L'Arche in 2020 concluded that Vanier had sexually abused numerous women over the course of several decades. There is no evidence that Nouwen knew anything about the abuse Vanier committed.

22. Nouwen describes his transformation in his autobiographical book, *The Road to Daybreak: A Spiritual Journey* (New York: Image, 1998).

23. Corrie ten Boom with John and Elizabeth Sherrill, *The Hiding Place* (Old Tappan, New Jersey: Fleming H. Revell Company, 1971), 217.

24. For more on The Parents Circle—Family Forum, see www.TheParentsCircle.org.

25. Eve Fairbanks, "I Have Sinned against the Lord and against You! Will You Forgive Me?," *New Republic*, June 18, 2014, https://newrepublic.com/article/118135/adriaan-vlok-ex-apartheid-leader-washes-feet-and-seeks-redemption.

26. Wilma Derksen, *Letting Go: One Woman's Walk to Forgiveness* (Grand Rapids: Zondervan, 2017), 28.

27. Julian of Norwich, *Showings,* translated by Edmund Colledge and James Walsh (New York: Paulist Press, 1978), 190.

28. Julian of Norwich, 225.

29. Julian of Norwich, 183.

30. James Loney, *Captivity: 118 Days in Iraq and the Struggle for a World without War* (Toronto: Knopf, 2011), 113.

The Author

Carol Penner has served as a pastor and chaplain and is an assistant professor and director of the theological studies program at Conrad Grebel University College in Waterloo, Ontario. She is the author of *Every Day Worship* and *Healing Waters: Churches Working to End Violence against Women* and the coeditor of *Resistance: Confronting Violence, Power, and Abuse in Peace Churches*. She writes and speaks about worship, including for *Rejoice!* and *Canadian Mennonite* and on her worship blog, LeadingInWorship.com.